Planning
BLENDED
Worship

Robert E. Webber

Planning BLENDED Worship

The Creative Mixture of Old and New

ABINGDON PRESS
NASHVILLE

PLANNING BLENDED WORSHIP
The Creative Mixture of Old and New

Copyright © 1998 by Abingdon Press

This book is printed on recycled, acid-free paper.

Library of Congress Cataloging-in-Publication Data

Webber, Robert.
    Planning blended worship : the creative mixture of old and new / Robert E. Webber.
        p.   cm.
    Includes bibliographical references.
    ISBN 0-687-03223-7 (paper : adhesive-bound)
    1. Public worship.   I. Title.
BV15.W385   1998
264—dc21   98-39716
                                                                          CIP

Unless otherwise noted, Scripture quotations are from the HOLY BIBLE, NEW INTERNATIONAL VERSION®. Copyright © 1973, 1978, 1984 by the International Bible Society. Used by permission of Zondervan Bible Publishers.

Scripture quotations noted NRSV are from the New Revised Standard Version Bible, copyright © 1989, by the Division of Christian Education of the National Council of the Churches of Christ in the United States of America.

Scripture quotations noted RSV are from the Revised Standard Version Bible, copyright 1946, 1952, 1971 by the Division of Christian Education of the National Council of the Churches of Christ in the USA. Used by permission.

Scripture quotations noted KJV are from the King James Version Bible.

00 01 02 03 04 05 06 07—10 9 8 7 6 5 4

MANUFACTURED IN THE UNITED STATES OF AMERICA

Acknowledgments

The writing of any book is influenced by a number of people, many of whom never receive any acknowledgment. I owe a debt of gratitude to the scholarly work done by a considerable number of liturgists and worship renewalists. I have read and studied their writings, ingesting into my own thinking their labor of love for worship. I have also benefited tremendously from numerous worship leaders in local churches who have dared to risk experimentation within their own worship services; some of these ventures have failed, but some have survived and will continue to have life into the twenty-first century. Thank you to all those unnamed people whose research and work finds expression in this book.

I also owe a debt of gratitude to my editors at Abingdon, who first suggested that I write this book. Their confidence and trust in my ability was a constant companion of hope.

A note of appreciation belongs to Arik Berglund, my teaching assistant at Wheaton College Graduate School. His abilities as a writer and editor are reflected in the flow and content of the text.

Contents

Tables

Introduction

*The greatest challenges, as well as the greatest returns, will come
to those churches that manage to bring both tendencies together
(traditional and contemporary worship) in creative ways, that
incarnate an ancient future faith.*

L. SWEET, FAITHQUAKES (P. 48)

The Future of Christian Worship

The present revolution in worship needs to be understood against the background of the historical progression
of worship since the seventeenth and eighteenth centuries.
During that time worship was primarily pedagogical. People met around the Word. They sang the Psalms, read the
Word, listened to sermons, and then discussed the implica-
tions of the Word of God for their lives and contemporary
society. This Word-driven approach to worship was swept
away by the rise of the evangelistic approach introduced by
Charles Finney and his "New Means." By the end of the
nineteenth century, the evangelistic service, with its climac-
tic altar call, was the dominant model of worship in most
free churches.

After 1950, the evangelistic model went through some
adjustments because of the shift toward a more highly edu-
cated ministry. A hybrid model emerged which combined
the order of evangelistic worship with a teaching sermon.
In many cases, the altar call was either dropped completely
or remodeled into an invitation that took place without any

outward decision required by congregation members. By the 1980s, however, the hybrid model came under increased scrutiny. Its relevance was called into question by the rise of a more dynamic approach to worship.

During the gradual evolution of contemporary worship models, the Western world came crashing through the post–World War II era into what is now known as the age of postmodernity. A primary factor in the worldview shift of the past half century has been the crumbling of the Enlightenment (or Modern) consensus with its positivist emphasis on reason, observation, and individualism. The Western world has been shifting toward a more dynamic, mixed philosophy of life with an emphasis on mystery, experience, and community. A new supernaturalism of an ancient pagan sort emerged with its unabashed mystical orientation: the New Age movement. Toward the end of the twentieth century this shift began to appear most vividly in films like George Lucas's *Star Wars,* with its mystical religion of the "Force," and in Steven Spielberg's *E.T.,* which carried definitive overtones of an otherworld reality.

Meanwhile, the entire world was undergoing a new globalization, primarily as the result of the communication revolution. The changing world was deposited nightly in everyone's living room and became a constant dinner companion for millions. The Berlin Wall fell, and with it began the disintegration of many other walls that separated peoples and societies. These shifts made an impact on the Church by softening theological differences and denominational distinctions that had previously separated churches from one another. The theological systems and denominational particulars that at one time divided one church from another have become increasingly blurred. The priority of a Christ-centered faith took precedence over theological rules and denominational confessions. Systematic theology gave way to historical theology; rigid structures of thought were replaced by relational faith.

Overall, a seismic shift occurred in the local church: In the past when Christians moved into town they asked, "Where's the best preaching?" Today, when Christians move to a new town they say, "Where's the best worship?" This transition from a sermon-driven service to a worship-driven service began emerging during the 1960s. What has happened since is nothing short of astounding. The Christian world has witnessed the rise of two worship renewal movements: the liturgical worship renewal and the new approach of contemporary worship.

Liturgical renewal began in the Roman Catholic Church with the promulgation of the Constitutions on the Sacred Liturgy in 1963. In the opening salvo of the groundbreaking council of Vatican II, the Tridentine Mass established during the Counter Reformation of the sixteenth century was overturned in favor of a new mass that revolutionized the content, structure, and style of Catholic worship. This Catholic worship renewal subsequently made a decisive impact on Protestant mainline churches. In the next thirty years every traditional denomination imitated the reforms of Vatican II by producing their own new worship books and hymnbooks. This revolution has been called "liturgical renewal," and like the renewal in Catholic worship, Protestant worship renewal has moved in the direction of recovering a worship characterized by biblical content and the fourfold structure of gathering together, hearing the Word, responding with thanksgiving, and being commissioned forth into the world. What has emerged in the Catholic and mainline Protestant churches is an ecumenical consensus on worship.

However, an entirely different approach to worship renewal emerged in the Pentecostal, charismatic, and praise and worship traditions. Their concern was to recover the more subjective and experiential side of worship. Pentecostals emphasized speaking in tongues, charismatics the gifts of the Spirit, while the praise and worship movement generated a new genre of music: the contemporary chorus. These churches introduced new instruments, such as the guitar, drums, and synthesizers, and new forms of communication, such as drama and congregational dance. Congregations became more involved in worship through uplifted hands, circles of prayer, and times of testimony. And ministry, which once belonged outside the worship service, became an integral part of worship, through the incorporation of such things as the laying on of hands and the rite of healing into the actual service.

The two movements of worship renewal, liturgical and contemporary, had independent histories until the 1990s when a form of blended or convergence worship began to develop. Blended worship draws from the biblical and historical sources that have faced the changes in traditional worship, but it has been equally concerned to draw from contemporary worship. For this reason blended worship is characterized by these three concerns: first, to be rooted in the biblical and early church tradition; second, to draw from the resources of the entire church; and third, a radical commitment to contemporary relevance. (See table A.)

TABLE A: TWENTIETH-CENTURY ROOTS OF WORSHIP RENEWAL

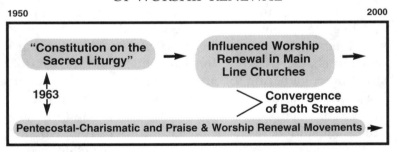

During the last decades of the twentieth century, two distinct approaches to worship renewal have emerged. First, Catholic and mainline renewal emphasized the recovery of a theology of worship, the fourfold biblical pattern, and a focus on God's transcendence. Second, the charismatic and praise and worship movement emphasized an experience of God during worship through an intimate encounter with God's presence. A convergence began about 1990 to blend these two streams: blended worship is characterized by synthesizing substance and relevance, traditional and contemporay forms.

As planners of worship think through the form and style of worship in their churches, it will be useful to keep in mind the ever-changing cultural context in which the Church lives and moves and has its being. In *Planning Blended Worship* these issues have been taken into consideration and suggestions have been made to traditional, contemporary, and blended churches that will help in planning a worship rooted in the past, yet deeply concerned for the present.

Eight Common Elements of Worship Renewal

Since 1963, the sources of worship renewal—investigation into the biblical roots of worship, studies in the historical models of worship, and the experimentation of contemporary churches—have resulted in a worship phenomena all around the world. This virtual explosion has matured enough for us to discern eight common elements.

1. Worship renewal is committed to draw from *biblical resources*. A new concern throughout the Church has been to recover a worship rooted in God's saving actions in history. New attention has been paid to the dynamic character of the God who has acted in history and who currently acts in our history. Worship renewal is occupied with the question, How does the God who acted in the past act now in our worship?

2. Worship renewal is characterized by *an interest in the worship traditions of the past*. There is a growing awareness that in order to move into the future we must do so on the basis of the past. This trend has resulted in a critical study of the immediate past (the last several hundred years of Protestant history) and a new appreciation of the worship of the ancient church—both Roman Catholic and Eastern Ortho-

dox. But the greatest amount of interest has been in the worship of the early Church, particularly in the first five centuries—the period of the common history of all Christians.

3. Worship renewal has generated *a new focus on Sunday worship.* In some churches worship seems rote, boring, and dead; singing is listless, preaching is dull, prayer seems monotonous, and the Lord's Supper has become like a funeral dirge. Since Sunday worship is the pinnacle event of the church week, pastors and congregations are awakening to the need to bring new life to the weekly Sunday event.

4. There has been a virtual explosion of *new music.* Music provides the emotional substance of worship. Since worship is now understood as a rehearsal of our relationship with God, music is seen as the wheels that move the gathering of the people into the presence of God; it helps congregations hear and respond to the word of God; it assists worshipers to encounter the living Christ at the Table, and it sends them forth into the world to love and serve the Lord. Gaining prominence is an eclectic use of music that draws from ancient hymns, Scripture songs, chants, and gospel and contemporary songs. The use of new kinds of instrumentation is also broadening—expanding from the sole use of the organ to the inclusion of piano, synthesizer, drums, guitar, percussion instruments, and brass and stringed instruments.

5. Renewalists have universally expressed an interest in *restoring the arts* to their rightful place in worship. Protestant worship began in the crucible of the Gutenberg Revolution, and historically it has always been primarily Word-driven. In the medieval era communication (and worship) was highly visual, but Protestantism rejected visual communication in favor of a more verbal approach to worship. Today, due to the new communication revolution, Protestantism is restoring the visual to worship.

6. Worship renewalists' recognition that worship is a cel-

ebration of the mighty deeds of God's salvation has caused a recovery of the service of *the Christian calendar*. In Advent we wait for the coming of the Messiah; at Christmas we celebrate his birth; at Epiphany we manifest his saving power to the whole world; at Lent we prepare to die with him; during Holy Week we do die with him; on Easter we are raised with him; and at Pentecost we experience the coming of the Holy Spirit who guides us into the future. This brief summary highlights the evangelical nature of the historical Christian calendar and its focus on the celebration of God's historical deeds of salvation.

7. A plethora of new studies have dealt with *the sacred actions of the Church*. The Christocentric focus of worship renewal has highlighted the two dominical sacraments of baptism and Eucharist; it has also developed a renewed appreciation of all the sacred actions of the Church. The ancient practice of baptism as a sacral ritual entrance into the Church is currently being restored, and the celebration of the resurrection in our worship is the renewing focus of the Communion Table. In the renewal of baptism and Eucharist, as well as in the sealing of the Spirit (confirmation), confession (reconciliation), marriage, ordination, and anointing, we recognize that these are not dead rituals, but sacred actions that communicate the presence of God among us.

8. Finally, interest has emerged to relate worship to *the ministries of the Church*. Worship does for the Church what God has done for us in Christ at the Cross and through the resurrection. It restores the relationship of individuals and the collective Church to God. Worship renewal is now recovering the ministerial offices that bring healing to our lives and compel us to reach out to others with a helping and comforting hand.

Planning Blended Worship concentrates primarily on the Sunday event and does not attempt to deal exhaustively with all eight areas of worship renewal. However, this book does demonstrate how each of these eight expressions of worship renewal pertain to the planning of the Sunday event.

Content, Structure, and Style

A helpful way to think about the planning of worship is to begin with the distinction between content, structure, and style. The content of Christian worship is unabashedly Trinitarian. Worship extols, blesses, and magnifies the eternal Father who is holy and transcendent and dwells in inaccessible light in the eternal kingdom of glory; it gives thanksgiving for the work of the Son through whom the world was created and has its being and in whom the world has been rescued by the mystery of the Incarnation, the power of the Cross, and the glory of the resurrection; it invokes the presence of the Holy Spirit, the Paraclete who comes alongside to teach, to admonish, and to guide us into truth. In this way the content of worship actualizes the Church, the body of Christ on earth, providing a brief foretaste of the future rule of God over all things. This kind of worship content forms a Christian worldview and empowers the Church to be a redeeming and reconciling influence in society.

The structure of worship most highly recommended is the fourfold pattern, which is rooted in Scripture and history, particularly the first six centuries of the Church. The description in Acts 2:42 of the earliest Christian worship recounts how early Christians gathered around the apostles' teaching and the breaking of bread in the context of prayer and fellowship. This passage provides evidence that from its inception, Christian worship had two primary focuses: Word and Table. To gather and to be sent forth established the fourfold worship pattern: Gathering, the Word, Thanksgiving, Dismissal. (See table B.)

TABLE B: THE FOURFOLD PATTERN OF WORSHIP

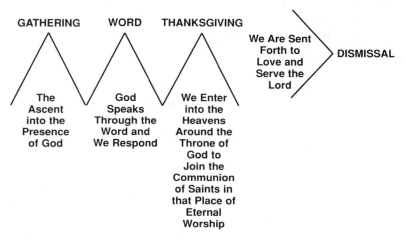

The fourfold pattern of worship is characterized by a narrative quality because it is taking us someplace (the throne room of God's kingdom) where a rehearsal of our relationship to God is expressed through the word and the response of thanksgiving. Having been touched God, we are sent forth into the world to love and serve the Lord. This fourfold pattern is the biblical and historical structure of worship that most effectively communicates the content of worship.

When the Gathering and the Dismissal are added it becomes clear that the model of early Christian worship was a fourfold pattern, and today there is a veritable universal consensus that the structure of worship should still continue to be this way. Yet while the content of worship (the gospel) is non-negotiable and the fourfold pattern of worship is strongly recommended, the style of worship is subject to considerable variety. This is because worshiping styles are rooted in the ever-changing kaleidoscope of human culture. There is no one style of worship that is suitable for all people always and everywhere. Instead, the style of worship will differ according to time and place relative to the changing patterns of culture.

For example, I attended a performance of Mozart's Mass in C Minor in a Chicago Episcopal church. The content of this mass was the gospel, and the structure followed the fourfold pattern. But the style was formal, with vestments, incense, processions, sung scripture lessons, and written prayers. Across town in a charismatic church pastored by a friend of mine, the same content and structure were being followed. The people sang for a full hour as they gathered for worship. Next the Scriptures were read, and the pastor preached for an hour. Following this they took an intermission and enjoyed a time of fellowship over coffee and doughnuts. Returning to their worship space again, they celebrated the Lord's Supper. Finally, the minister dismissed them with a benediction. Although the two styles of the high liturgical mass and the charismatic service were disparate, the content and structure of each were rooted in the same biblical and historical tradition. What differed was the style.

Style is not now, nor has ever been, a matter of biblical tradition. Whether our worship is formal, informal, or a combination of both, the style of worship depends on taste. Because the style of worship is the window to the church (or sometimes literally the window itself), we must allow our style to reflect who we are as a people. The Christian world is composed of many varieties of people; some worship best in a high liturgical style; some worship best in the contemporary setting of a chorus band. Others' tastes lie somewhere on the spectrum between the two. No one style is normative for all churches.

The Changing Style of Communication

One of the underlying issues in worship renewal is the need to return worship to the people. A passive approach to worship has slowly seeped into the Church over the past several centuries, and many contemporary Christians have grown up believing that worship is something *for* them, rather than something they *do* themselves. Our present situation is not unlike that of the Middle Ages when worship had become completely clericalized; the action of the worship service itself was happening in the chancel with the priests, the acolytes, the choir, and the musicians. A congregation's duty was to listen and watch. Even the Eucharist was seldom consumed. The Reformers knew it was wrong to take worship out of the hands of the congregation, so they sought to return worship to the pew. Unfortunately, Protestantism is now in the same situation that Roman Catholicism was in five centuries ago; it, too, has become clericalized and finds its worship services mired in passivity. Worship renewal for the twenty-first century, like the Reformation, seeks to declericalize worship and return it to the people.

An authentic encounter with the living God in worship will touch the whole person—the mind, the emotions, and the symbolic and intuitive dimensions of the person. Renewed worship is not made possible so much by the logic of propositions as by experiencing the story of Christianity together as a community. Renewed worship tells, enacts, sings, and experiences the stories of faith that define and empower the community to become a participant in the great drama of salvation.

Communication
Through Cultural Transmission

The oldest means of transmitting worldviews in the context of a community is through oral communication. Communication specialists call this form of communication "cultural transmission." Cultural transmission consists of the stories, symbols, and images that provide coherence and meaning to a particular community. The people of Israel communicated their faith orally; the stories of Creation, the Patriarchs, the Exodus Event, the

Judges, and the Prophets were all stories of faith passed down and experienced from generation to generation. The primary means through which these stories were handed down was the daily, weekly, and yearly feasts and fasts of the Jewish worship calendar. Faith was transmitted through their worship events, and through this enactment of worship the community was formed and shaped into the people of God.

The same can be said of the earliest Christian community. They were an oral community shaped not only by the stories and events of the Old Testament, but by the new stories of fulfillment. The kerygma of the New Testament is that the kingdom of God is at hand, the Messiah has come, and people now must repent, be baptized, and enter into the new community of Jesus Christ. The stories surrounding the birth, life, death, and resurrection of Christ, as well as the founding of the Church on the day of Pentecost, were all narrative foundations for this new community. The symbols of water, bread, and wine became the signs of ritual entrance and fellowship in this new community. All of these sacred actions were handed down in the context of community worship—events in which the community gathered to be formed and shaped through the telling of their stories and the enactment of their symbols.

For the first fifteen and a half centuries of the Church, cultural transmission was the primary means of the Church's communication. People were evangelized and nurtured into the faith through an immersion into the stories and images that were passed down in worship. The Church was a community, and members learned the language and worldview of the community in the same way they learned their mother tongue: through immersed participation. Faith was not taught systematically from published articles of belief; it was learned through cultural transmission.

The Era of Didactic Communication

Communication through cultural transmission was transformed significantly in the fifteenth century by the rise of print media. The Protestant Reformation was fueled by the Gutenberg Revolution, and subsequently it developed new methods of communication which thereafter dominated Western Christianity. Print media introduced a form of communication that was antagonistic to the participatory immersion of cultural transmission. Communication shifted from the community to the individual, from learning through participatory experience to didactic forms of teaching.

Protestant worship became didactic, and Protestant leaders purged their sanctuaries of all visual communications. Iconoclastic arguments were made against the use of all images and symbols. The Christian calendar year, with all of its traditional feasts and fasts, was abruptly denounced. Liturgies with procession and rich ceremonies of pomp and circumstance were brought to a halt. Symbols of immersed participation such as pilgrimages, street parades, and feast days were viewed as abhorrent. A new worship was born almost overnight, an almost exclusively verbal worship. The mind became the only receptor of truth, and nearly all visual forms of communication disappeared. In their place the new Church offered spartan space filled only by the spoken word.

The catechism became the primary form for the communication of the faith, becoming the greatest innovation for the spread of Christianity since the beginning of the Christian era. Luther's catechism sold more than 100,000 copies in the first forty years it was published. All other Protestant denominations, and even the Roman Catholic Church, followed suit and developed their own catechisms. Consequently, Christianity shifted its means of communicating faith from a primary emphasis on an immersed participatory experience of worship to an emphasis on learning through reading and listening to the Word of God. The Church and all its functions (including worship) became highly pedagogical.

Communication in an Audiovisual Society

Since 1950, a new communication revolution has been generated by the electronic media and by innovative, unprecedented ways of storing, processing, and communicating information. This audiovisual revolution has transformed the print-media society dramatically within the past few decades. The more didactic form of Christianity, which has developed since the time of Martin Luther, is now in jeopardy of facing extinction. The Church faces a new challenge as significant as the one introduced by the invention of the Gutenberg press. It must generate relevant means of communication that meet the demands of the new communication revolution. (See table C.)

The current communication revolution is a shift away from the didactic nature of the print media to a more experiential form of communication based, ironically, largely on participatory experience. This turn of events is, in a sense, a "reverse Reformation." Faith is no longer nourished exclusively by doctrine and intellectual speculation, but by imaginative immersion in participatory Christian communities.

This affective form of communication works best in the experience of a community held together by the mysteries of its stories, events, and symbols. Faith comes through sharing, through being loved, through a sense of connection, and through the celebration of those events that provide meaning to the community. This new, experiential method holds priority over doctrines and formulas of faith that explain and provide reasons for the faith. It does not contradict or nullify the faith of the Church; it simply communicates it in a more personal manner. This shift in the communication of faith will find expression in numerous parts of the Church, especially where community is an

TABLE C: ENLIGHTENMENT COMMUNICATION

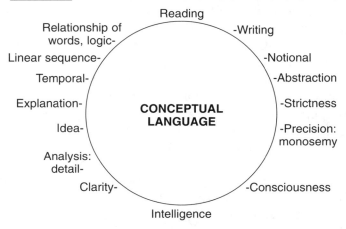

Reading
Relationship of words, logic-
-Writing
Linear sequence-
-Notional
Temporal-
-Abstraction
Explanation-
CONCEPTUAL LANGUAGE
-Strictness
Idea-
-Precision: monosemy
Analysis: detail-
Clarity-
-Consciousness
Intelligence

POST-ENLIGHTENMENT COMMUNICATION

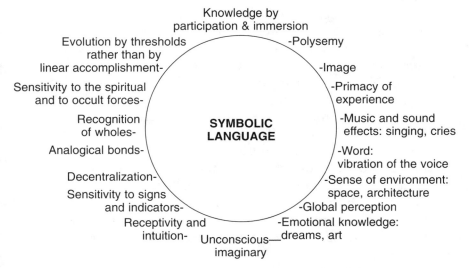

Knowledge by participation & immersion
Evolution by thresholds rather than by linear accomplishment-
-Polysemy
-Image
Sensitivity to the spiritual and to occult forces-
-Primacy of experience
Recognition of wholes-
SYMBOLIC LANGUAGE
-Music and sound effects: singing, cries
Analogical bonds-
-Word: vibration of the voice
Decentralization-
-Sense of environment: space, architecture
Sensitivity to signs and indicators-
-Global perception
Receptivity and intuition-
-Emotional knowledge: dreams, art
Unconscious—imaginary

The form of communications that dominated the Enlightenment and affected the worship of the church was that of conceptual language. The new form of communication of the Post-Enlightenment world is that of symbolic language. (Used with permission of Pierre Babin, *The New Era in Religious Communication* [Minneapolis: Fortress Press, 1991], pp. 150-51.)

essential factor: the family, the local church, small groups, praise marches, and pilgrimages to new holy places, such as the Taize community in France. These are experiences that confirm faith and establish Christian commitment.

Because of our new cultural situation, the greatest moments of vulnerability for faith are those life situations that represent transformation and change: passages such as marriage, divorce, and retirement; turning points such as the deaths of loved ones, the loss of employment, or injuries to physical or mental health. These are moments in life that affect the heart directly—times when worship experiences must be facilitated to meet a society that no longer functions according to didactic communication methods. The old methods need to be supplanted by new communication modes that generate atmospheres of warmth, love, and healing (methods of communication aimed at cultural transmission).

The current communication revolution obviously raises questions about the future of the Church. How can we expect a positive future for Christianity if it returns to a form of communication that was all but stamped out by the Reformation? Form is an agent of message. The Church must learn to distinguish between the *message* of faith and the *form* in which it is communicated. Late medieval Christianity experienced a corruption of its message through the accretion of numerous cultural additions to the faith. The Reformers repudiated both the corrupted message and the form in which it was communicated. The cultural changes being introduced by contemporary communication calls Christians to find new wineskins for an unchanging wine. Consequently, it is not the historic content of worship that needs to change but the form and style that delivers the content.

While spiritual knowing is ultimately a gift of grace from God, there are means by which we can facilitate spiritual knowing. For example, the hospitality of church people can communicate faith to those whose hearts are open to receive what God has for them. The aim of this book is to focus on the entire service of worship as not only the window to the local church, but also as a window to the heart. In contemporary society the heart is reached through *participation*, and all approaches to worship—traditional, contemporary, or blended—need to relearn how to achieve services characterized by immersed participation.

The New Paradigm:
Worship Is the Center of the Hourglass

It is fair to say that worship renewal is creating a paradigm shift in the local church. In the seventeenth and eighteenth centuries the local church was seen as a school, and worship was primarily aimed at educating the mind. With the nineteenth-century shift introduced by the rise of mass evangelism, the local church became an "evangelistic tent," and worship became the means of calling sinners to repentance and faith. Currently there is a growing awareness that worship is the central ministry of the Church: Worship is the center of the hourglass, the key to forming the inner life of the Church. Everything the Church does moves toward public worship, and all its ministries proceed from worship. Good worship creates community, evangelical warmth, hospitality to outsiders, inclusion of cultural diversity, leadership roles for men and women, intergenerational involvement, personal and community formation, healing, reconciliation, and other aspects of pastoral care. Because worship is itself an act of witness, it is the door to church growth, to missions and evangelism, and to issues of social justice. Worship now stands at the center of the Church's life and mission in the world.

Let me give you a good example of a new paradigm church. About ten years ago, this church had a small handful of people, but they committed themselves to being a community concerned for the healing of hurts, particularly for people with damaged emotions. They began a Wednesday night healing service celebrated in the context of a written liturgy, and as word went out, more and more people came to this church to find stability, transcendence, and intimacy in the healing prayers and the touch of the laying on of hands.

Sunday morning worship was ordered around the fourfold pattern of worship with a free use of *The Book of Common Prayer*. The liturgy came to belong to the congregation, as artists in the field of visuals, drama, music, and technology began to find their ministry in the church. Processions are filled with drama, color, and movement as the congregation joyfully enters into the heavenly place of worship. The music of the liturgy draws from the hymns of the early Church, from chants, Reformation hymns, the music of Isaac Watts, gospel songs, African American spirituals, and from other contemporary choruses. Scriptures are read sometimes with musical accompaniment, sometimes with pantomime, but always with clarity and conviction. Sermons are based on the scripture readings, and the preaching tends to be narrative and story-formed. Prayers are recited by the entire congregation. The passing of the peace is a holy bedlam; people embrace each other with joyous acclamations and personal warmth. The Eucharist is celebrated every Sunday; the bread and cup are lifted with great enthusiasm, and as people come to receive the bread and wine, the community breaks forth into songs remembering the crucifixion and celebrating the resurrection. Throughout the Eucharist service, appointed laypersons anoint worshipers with oil and offer up prayers of healing on their behalf. And finally, recessionals are joyous experiences of being sent forth into the world as God's light.

And who comes to this church? *Every* age group is represented, but it is decidedly a church of the present generation. Ask these young people why they love their church and they will talk about community, transcendence, intimacy, participation, pageantry, and musical variety; most of all they will talk about how the gospel touches them, heals them, and makes them whole. This church is now over one thousand members strong and still growing vibrantly; they have shown that it is possible "to do church" *and* act as a community that cares. There is a place in this world for a hospitable church, for a church that combines full worship with a desire to minister to others. This is the church of the future, the new paradigm emerging for the next century.

A Guide to Determining Your Worship Profile

1. Study table A. Which of the following categories best describes your church?

Affected by Catholic and mainline worship renewal

Affected by the pentecostal, charismatic, or praise and worship renewal

Affected by the movement to blend traditional and contemporary worship

Not affected by any of the worship renewal movements

2. Identify the age make up of the people in your church.

_____% of people in our church are boosters (born before 1945).

_____% of people in our church are boomers (born between 1945 and 1961).

_____% of people in our church are from generation X (born after 1961).

3. Of the 8 common elements of worship renewal, which ones

have made an impact on the worship of your church? Evaluate each of the areas on a scale of 1 (least impact) to 10 (most impact). Then take time to discuss those areas that are weakest.

a) Our church draws from a biblical understanding of worship.

   1   2   3   4   5   6   7   8   9   10

b) The worship of our church draws from the past, especially the early church.

   1   2   3   4   5   6   7   8   9   10

c) Our church has experienced a new focus on Sunday worship.

   1   2   3   4   5   6   7   8   9   10

d) Our church draws from the music of the whole church.

   1   2   3   4   5   6   7   8   9   10

e) Our church has restored the use of the arts.

   1   2   3   4   5   6   7   8   9   10

f) Our church follows the calendar of the Christian year effectively.

   1   2   3   4   5   6   7   8   9   10

g) Our church has experienced the restoration of life in the sacred actions of worship.

   1   2   3   4   5   6   7   8   9   10

h) The worship of our church empowers its outreach ministries.

   1   2   3   4   5   6   7   8   9   10

4. Evaluate the content, structure, and style of your worship. Again, use a scale of 1 ("That does not describe our church at all.") to 10 ("Yes, that is our church!"). Discuss areas of greatest weakness.

a) The content of our worship is the full story of scripture.

1   2   3   4   5   6   7   8   9   10

b) The structure of our worship is the universally accepted fourfold pattern.

1   2   3   4   5   6   7   8   9   10

c) The style of our worship is appropriate to our congregation and to the people we attract.

1   2   3   4   5   6   7   8   9   10

5. Study table C and answer the following:

a) The approach to worship in our church is based upon:

Conceptual language

Symbolic language

b) The communication style of our church will relate best to:
Boosters

Boomers

Generation X

All of the above

6. I would describe our church as:

An old paradigm church

A new paradigm church

7. Draw from each of the previous questions to create a worship profile of the church. Do so by completing each of the following sentences:

a) Our church has been affected by (which stream of worship renewal)

_____

_____ .

b) Our age group is primarily _____ .

c) Of the eight aspects of worship renewal we draw on

_____ .

d) The content of our worship is

_____ .

e) The structure of our worship is

_____ .

f) The style of our worship is

_____ .

g) Our approach to communication is

_____ .

8. To complete this study, comment on the kinds of changes you would like to see occur in the worship of your church.

Chapter 1

The Content of Worship:
The Triune God

You are God: we praise you;
You are the Lord: we acclaim you;
You are the eternal Father:
All creation worships you.
To you all angels, all the powers of heaven,
Cherubim and seraphim sing in endless praise:
  Holy, holy, holy Lord, God of power and might,
  heaven and earth are full of your glory.
The glorious company of apostles praise you.
The noble fellowship of prophets praise you.
The white-robed army of martyrs praise you.
Throughout the whole world the holy church acclaims you;
  Father, of majesty unbounded,
  your true and only Son, worthy of all worship,
  and the Holy Spirit, advocate and guide.
You, Christ, are the king of glory,
the eternal Son of the Father.
When you became man to set us free
you did not shun the Virgin's womb.
You overcame the sting of death
and opened the kingdom of heaven to all believers.
You are seated at God's right hand in glory.
We believe that you will come and be our judge.
  Come then, Lord, and help your people,
  bought with the price of your own blood,
  and bring us with your saints
  to glory everlasting.

TE DEUM (FOURTH CENTURY) FROM THE BOOK OF COMMON PRAYER

Defining Worship

Some time ago I was talking to a good friend who had just returned from conducting a weekend workshop on worship. When I asked him what they had spent the weekend discussing, he told me they were brainstorming a definition of worship. "All worship planning must begin with a definition of worship," he said. His statement is exactly the place where *Planning Blended Worship* needs to begin.

There is no finer definition of worship than Te Deum (Latin for "You are God"). It is a prayer that dates from the fourth century and represents a high point in the development of a theology of worship. Although the origin of the prayer cannot be traced, the content of the prayer and its understanding of worship are rooted in scripture and in the development of early Christian thought. The themes of God's transcendence, God's glory in creation, and God's actions throughout salvation history are all found in the writings and liturgies of the early Church fathers.

Te Deum is a prayer, and this fact calls attention to the forgotten reality that worship is primarily prayer. Worship is a prayer of relationship in which the whole creation lauds and magnifies God, the Creator and Redeemer of the world. Unfortunately, many congregations do not envision worship as a prayer; instead, worship is seen merely as a kind of fellowship, outreach, edification, or healing. Te Deum bids us acknowledge what Kierkegaard once noted, that if there is an audience in worship, it is God. Te Deum calls us to rid ourselves of the language of stage, audience, and performance. Worship is a dramatic expression of God's glory and a representation of God's saving deeds in history.

A second key to worship expressed by Te Deum is that there is a place where worship is eternally happening. That place is in the heavens, and when we worship we join the heavenly throng, the angels and archangels, the cherubim and the seraphim, and the whole company of saints—the prophets, the apostles, and the martyrs. Jesus alludes to an eternal place of worship in his conversation with the Samaritan woman: "A time is coming when you will worship the Father neither on this mountain nor in Jerusalem . . . when the true worshipers will worship the Father in spirit and truth" (John 4:21, 23). Repudiating the common Jewish places of worship, Jesus locates the place of worship in the Spirit. He refers to the eternal place of worship around the throne where continual worship is offered to God. When we worship, we ascend into the heavens and join heavenly worship, as did Isaiah:

> In the year that King Uzziah died, I saw the Lord seated on the throne, high and exalted, and the train of his robe filled the temple. Above him were seraphs, each with six wings. With two wings they covered their faces, with two they covered their feet, and with two they were flying. And they were calling to one another,
> "Holy, holy, holy is the LORD Almighty;
> the whole earth is full of his glory."
> At the sound of their voices the doorposts and thresholds shook and the temple was filled with smoke. (Isaiah 6:1-4)

In the New Testament, John wrote of a similar experience: "On the Lord's Day I was *in the Spirit* [the heavenly place]" (Revelation 1:10); "At once I was *in the Spirit*, and there before me was a throne in heaven with someone sitting on it" (Revelation 4:2). The whole book of Revelation is primarily about worship and the praise that belongs to God because of God's ultimate overthrow of the powers of evil: "Worthy is the Lamb, who was slain, to receive power and wealth and wisdom and strength and honor and glory and praise!" (Revelation 5:12). The liturgies of the early Church follow this pattern of entering into heavenly worship, particularly at the Eucharist when the congregation joins the heavenly throng to sing *The Sanctus* and to recall God's mighty deeds of salvation.

Te Deum also teaches us that the worship of God is not the worship of an Essence that simply sits in the heavens. It is the worship of a God who not only creates, but becomes personally involved in creation. Worshiping God as the Creator is an essential part of worship; the Psalms are full of such Creator praise (see Psalms 8, 19, 65, 104, and 148). Following in the tradition of the Psalms, the liturgy of the synagogue and early Christian worship was also full of Creator praise. Worship also celebrates God's actions in history, whereby the created order was rescued after the Fall. God's saving acts—through Abraham and Sarah; Moses and Miriam; the prophets and prophetesses; Elizabeth and Mary; and ultimately, in the Incarnation, Crucifixion, and Resurrection—are all crucial to the message of salvation. Worship also declares that salvation history belongs not only to the past, but to the future as well. God will come in Jesus Christ to destroy all the powers of evil and to establish a new heaven and a new earth.

In worship we ascend into the heavens and join the heavenly hosts to proclaim the glory of God, to acclaim God as Creator, to remember God's mighty deeds of salvation, and to anticipate God's final victory over evil and the establishment of God's eternal kingdom. Through the words and actions of worship, the world is "realigned"; the order of Creation, from Creator to created, is established in its intended form. This is the essence of worship as understood by the early Church and which, if recovered today, has the power to revolutionize our worship and change the modern Church.

Understanding Worship Renewal

While biblical worship proclaims and enacts all of God's deeds, the source and fountainhead of worship is God's primordial act of salvation. For the Hebrew people God's saving event was the Exodus. For Christians, God's saving deed is the Christ Event: the Incarnation, the Crucifixion, and the Resurrection of Jesus.

For Jews the Exodus was important because God delivered them from their slavery and brought them to Mount Sinai and there entered into covenant relationship with them. By this action Yahweh became their God, and they Yahweh's people. Today, more than three thousand years later, Jews all over the world worship God at Passover by reenacting this covenant event. This event is the centerpiece of all Jewish worship.

Christians have always viewed the Exodus Event as a precursor to the Christ Event—the second Exodus, as it were. The entire world was in bondage to evil, having fallen into a self-imposed slavery to sin and death. The entire world was in need of deliverance. But God did not abandon us to our sin. God came to us in the Incarnation of Jesus Christ. The New Testament proclaims that God was reconciled with the world through the Christ Event (2 Corinthians 5:19); through Jesus Christ, God bound the powers of evil (Matthew 12:22-29), dethroned these powers (Colossians 2:15), and will ultimately destroy them at the end of history (Revelation 20–22). This event is the source of all Christian worship.

When Christians gather for worship, they declare God's glory and remember, proclaim, and enact the biblical story of God's ultimate rescuing of humanity through Jesus Christ. A passage that captures this essence of Christian worship is given to us by Peter: "You are a chosen race, a royal priesthood, a holy nation, God's own people, *in order that you may proclaim the mighty acts of him who called you out of darkness into his marvelous light*" (1 Peter 2:9 NRSV, italics mine).

What happens when we proclaim and enact God's mighty deeds of salvation? Two things happen: first, there is a divine action from above. Second, there is a human response from below. This is the heart of Christian worship. We now examine the two sides of "worship dialogue" to focus more clearly on the content of worship.

Divine Action Through Historical Recitation

The eternal worship in the heavens is Christ-centered. Revelation 4 and 5 reveals how the heavenly throng praises God for creation (4:11), for redemption (5:9-10, 12), and for the re-creation of all things (5:13-14). It is Jesus Christ who is at the very center of this praise because he has "opened the kingdom of heaven" (Te Deum). When we worship we enter into his kingdom, his rule over the entire creation. Here we sing the praises of the One who is seated at God's right hand glory. What lies at the heart of our praise is God's work of salvation in history through Jesus Christ, for he is the one who "became man to set us free," who "overcame the sting of death," who "will come and be our judge" and will "bring us with your saints to glory everlasting" (Te Deum). In earthly worship, we join heavenly worship and proclaim God's worth through the recitation of God's saving deeds in Jesus Christ.

This idea of historical recitation is captured by a prayer I heard once in a local church:

Lord, we bless you for creating us in your image. And we thank you that after we fell away into sin you did not leave us in our sin, but came to us in the person of Jesus Christ, who lived among us, died on our behalf, was resurrected for our salvation, ascended into heaven, and now sits at your right hand. We await your coming again to restore the created order. Bless us as we worship in your name. Amen.

This prayer captures the essence of biblical worship. It summarizes the whole story of salvation from creation to re-creation. The emphasis is not on the experience of the worshiper, but on God, who initiated a saving action toward creation, which was in desperate need of restoration. The history of the Bible is the continual tale of God maintaining and repairing a relationship with humanity. This salvation story is proclaimed, recalled, and enacted every time we worship.

A second illustration will help to make this more clear. I was in a church some time ago, and the congregation was asked to reflect in silence on a psalm that started off with the theme "my life is falling apart." After groaning about his plight, the psalmist began to reflect on the Exodus Event and God's saving action in history. When the writer finally came to the realization that the God who worked to deliver Israel could work in his present condition, the psalmist broke forth into praise.

A brief interpretation of the psalmist's experience will help us understand what happens in worship. First, the psalmist was aware of his *dislocation* in life. His life was in disarray. He was in a state of despair and confusion. Next, as the writer reflected on the memory of God's action in history and realized that God was for him, he became *relocated* in God and finally burst forth into praise. The underlying conviction of Christian worship is that we are all in a state of dislocation. We are dislocated from God, from self, from neighbor, and from nature. But God has entered into our history in Jesus Christ to bring relocation.

A third illustration may make this experience even more clear. Several years ago, William Allan Farmer, an African American songwriter and worship leader, came to Wheaton College to speak during the student body chapel. His first sermon was taken from a phrase in the Hebrew Scriptures, "Our God is an awesome God." He began by asking, "How do you know God is an awesome God?" After a pregnant pause he said, "You know God is an awesome God when you recite God's great saving deeds in history." And then

41

he said, "You will never go to an African American church without hearing a recitation of God's saving deeds." He followed this with an impromptu example:

> There were the children of Israel in bondage to pharaoh, making bricks without straw. And they cried to God to come and deliver them. And God sent Moses, who liberated them with signs and wonders. And there were Shadrach, Meshach, and Abednego in the fiery furnace, and God became present to them in their hour of distress and delivered them. Then there was Daniel in the lion's den, and God met him there, shut the mouths of the lions, and delivered him.

The point is that divine action happens through the recitation of God's saving deeds. When we in our worship hear of God's action in the past, we interpret God's past action to apply to our present dislocation. We begin thinking, "I am with Israel" or "I am in the fiery furnace" or "The lions are out to get me, too." The recitation of God's mighty saving deeds plays a central role in worship. We join the heavenly throng, and we sing or preach or enact God's mighty deeds of salvation which flow out from God's character, particularly God's loving-kindness.

Worship planners need to be guided by three central questions as they consider the content of worship:

1. How does this worship speak to God's glory in heaven and God's saving actions on earth?
2. How does this worship help people identify their dislocation?
3. How does this worship lead people into a relocation with God?

Because worship extols God by remembering the stories of God's saving deeds, the Bible frequently summarizes God's saving action in creedal form (see Deuteronomy

26:5-9). The New Testament provides us with a marvelous summary of God's action in Christ (see 1 Timothy 3:16 and 1 Corinthians 15:1-8). Many of the Psalms are also summaries of God's saving action (see Psalms 107 and 136). When we recite or sing creeds or creedlike hymns and choruses we are remembering God's saving action.

Biblical hymns were also written so that God's people could remember God's saving deeds. For example, the songs of Moses and Miriam in Exodus 15 recount and rejoice in the deliverance of Israel from the hands of Pharaoh. In the New Testament we find the beautiful hymn recorded by Paul describing how God became one of us and how in the end of history every knee shall bow and every tongue confess that Jesus Christ is Lord (Philippians 2:6-11). These stories and hymns are the memories of faith, the very stuff of worship! (See also John 1:1-4 and Colossians 1:13-22. These are identified by scholars as Christ hymns of the early Church.) When we sing hymns, we are singing the stories of our faith that are rooted in the memory of God's saving action.

Biblical worship is also very dramatic by nature. For example, during Passover Jews dramatize their redemption from Egypt by paying great attention to detail in dress, food, movement, and gesture (see Exodus 12). In a sense they are trying to literally reenact the Exodus Event. Similarly, when Christians gather at the Lord's Table to remember Christ's death and Resurrection, we are lifted into the heavens where we not only say words but add actions to them. We gather around the table; we break the bread; we lift the cup; we partake; we drink. With all these motions we actively remember God's saving deeds in history through the Christ Event.

When we gather to worship we are celebrating the most important events in human history—the events through which God brought salvation to the world. Through our celebration these historical events become contemporary to

43

us. In exactly the same way the Jewish people celebrate their liberation from Egypt, the Church celebrates its salvation in Christ through hymns and songs, Scripture reading and sermons, the creed, and the prayer of thanksgiving over bread and wine. As we celebrate God's saving deeds from the past and apply them to our present dislocation, the Holy Spirit brings God's past actions of deliverance into a present reality in our experience.

The Worshipers Respond to Divine Action

The memory and rehearsal of God's saving action is the divine side to worship. The other side to worship is our response. We are called to respond to God's past and present saving action with praise and thanksgiving. Let me illustrate. A study of God's saving deeds quickly demonstrates that the response of God's people is always praise and thanksgiving. Ponder, for example, the response of the patriarch Jacob who built a stone monument in response to God's action on his behalf (Genesis 35:14). Examine Israel's response to God's rescue from Egypt in the praise of Moses and Miriam's songs (Exodus 15:1-21). Reflect on the Psalms as a response of praise to God's action (Psalm 136). Recall the worship that surrounded the rebuilding of the temple when God brought Israel back from exile (Nehemiah 8:1-18). In New Testament times, praise accompanied the Incarnation (Luke 1–2), the Transfiguration (Matthew 17:1-13), and the Resurrection (Luke 2:21-22).

Praise and thanksgiving are the hallmark of our worship. We acclaim God as we enter God's presence; we laud God in response to the Scriptures that retell God's work on our behalf; we send up prayers of thanksgiving at the Table of the Lord; we go forth into the world to magnify God not only with our lips, but also with our lives.

The praise that we offer to God should result in a feeling of awe and wonder. When we worship we are encountering the indescribably holy God who created the entire universe and all its magisterial wonder.

As Isaiah discovered, worship that experiences the otherness of God will also result in the confession of our sinful condition. Isaiah's description of his experience with the living God gets at the heart of our approach to God's presence. One does not waltz carelessly into the presence of the Holy One. After all, God is God. No matter how good we feel about ourselves or our accomplishments, we are fallen creatures in need of God. To be in God's presence is to see ourselves for what we really are. It requires that we throw ourselves upon God's mercy and grace. This is what Isaiah did, and God spoke comforting, merciful words to him, assuring him that he was forgiven and loved. We need to hear those words from God, but we first must present ourselves to God with total humility.

It is imperative for planners of renewed worship to keep in mind that worship is a dialogue between God and the congregation. Worship is not a program of isolated acts of worship. It is a narrative, a retelling of the story of our relationship with God in history, past and present. Rightly understood, worship is a dynamic process that culminates in a rehearsal of our relationship with God. Worship planners need to give careful attention to the content of worship and to the response of praise and thanksgiving, for in this action true worship happens. And in true worship our relationship to God is established, maintained, repaired, and transformed.

The Divine-Human Encounter

The fourfold pattern of worship is the process through which the ordering of divine action and of the worshipers' response is accomplished externally. Several guidelines will help maximize the worshipers' experience through the fourfold pattern of worship. The first is the need to worship with *intention*. Any church's worship is only a formal, empty ritual if the worshipers do not respond with intentionality. Intention in worship is achieved when the heart knows its need and becomes open and vulnerable to God's action through a virtual abandonment. An abandoned spirit listens for God's Word to speak into the individual's own life.

Another guideline for the worshiper is to set free the imagination. Worship is an imaginative event which brings us before the very throne of God. As Revelation 4 and 5 suggest, we are raised into the heavens ourselves to worship with the angels, the archangels, the cherubim and seraphim, and the whole company of saints who forever sing, "Holy, holy, holy is the Lord God Almighty, who was, and is, and is to come." Care should be taken to touch all of the human senses during the worship service.

Finally, human response comes through the use of the body in worship. A principle at work in body language is that external order organizes internal experience. We can do nothing without our bodies. We greet people in our bodies, we go to work in our bodies, we express leisure in our bodies. The spirit within always tells the body what to do. In similar manner, we come to worship in our bodies, and the spirit within tells the body to be at worship. Consequently, when we stand, sit, kneel, raise our hands, or bow down, the body is at worship. Posture and movement in worship allows the whole person to be engaged in worship. Consequently, to stand for the Gathering, to sit for the Word, to kneel for Communion, to raise hands in signing, to do the sign of the cross, to genuflect, or to lie prostrate on the floor before the presence of God (as is being increasingly done in some churches) is to worship with the body in a way that communicates a relationship with the Divine. (See table D.)

In summary, worship is a Divine-human encounter in which the God of creation works in our personal lives, our

TABLE D: GESTURES OF WORSHIP

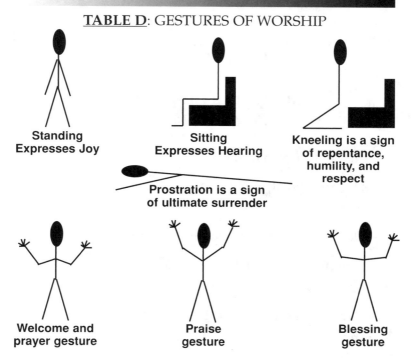

Standing
Expresses Joy

Sitting
Expresses Hearing

Kneeling is a sign
of repentance,
humility, and
respect

Prostration is a sign
of ultimate surrender

Welcome and
prayer gesture

Praise
gesture

Blessing
gesture

Encourage all the worshipers to make these gestures as a unitive body. Hands may be extended during intercessorary prayer, raised for songs of praise, extended to bless one another. All may kneel for a confession and also for the prayer of thanksgiving over bread and wine. These postures, when done with intention, communicate deep emotional content and arouse the feelings into an experience of worship.

families, our communities of faith, and in all of world history. This continued divine action happens as we join heavenly worship where God's person and action are eternally praised. We join that heavenly throng and worship with awe and wonder through an intentional abandonment, the unleashing of the imagination, and the free and open use of the body. This is worship as understood in the classical tradition of the Christian faith. As we turn now to a study of the structure of worship, I will show how the content of worship and the accompanying experience of the worshiper is ordered by the fourfold pattern, for the Holy Spirit uses the structure of worship to deliver the content and shape the worshiper's experience.

Guidelines for Planning the Content of Worship

1. Study Te Deum and answer the following questions:

—Describe what is happening in the heavenly place of worship.

—Describe the earthly place of worship.

—Comment on the Trinitarian nature of worship. Why is the Father worshiped? the Son? the Spirit?

—Identify the content of the historical recitation in worship.

2. Take a recent bulletin of your worship service (or prayer book or worship leader's outline and notes) and evaluate the content using the following:

—In what specific ways was the Triune nature of worship expressed?

—Identify all the expressions of historical recitation. Was the story of God's work in history (past and present) adequately expressed?

—How did this worship help the worshipers identify their dislocation? How did worship relocate the worshiper in God?

—Where did this worship create the feelings of awe and wonder in the worshiper?

—Was your worship a program? a narrative?

—In this worship, where were the following experienced: intention? imagination? the uses of the body?

3. Plan the content of an upcoming service of worship using these questions:

—How will your worship express the relationship between earthly and heavenly worship?

—How will your worship reflect the Triune nature of God?

—How will you recount the story of God's saving acts in history?

—How will the worship you have planned interface with the needs of people present?

Chapter 2

The Gathering: The Ascent into God's Presence

Glory to God in the highest,
 and peace to his people on earth.
Lord God, heavenly King,
almighty God and Father,
 we worship you, we give you thanks,
 we praise you for your glory.
Lord Jesus Christ, only Son of the Father,
Lord God, Lamb of God,
you take away the sin of the world:
 have mercy on us;
you are seated at the right hand of the Father:
 receive our prayer.
For you alone are the Holy One,
you alone are the Lord,
you alone are the Most High,
 Jesus Christ,
 with the Holy Spirit,
 in the glory of God the Father. Amen.

GLORIA IN EXCELSIS DEO, A FOURTH-CENTURY HYMN

The Nature of the Gathering

Worship always begins with an ascent into the presence of God. The shape of the ascent in Christian worship follows the Old Testament pattern of the entrance into Jerusalem, expressed in the psalms of ascent. Consequently, the nature of the Gathering is shaped by an upward movement as God's earthly people travel toward the heavenly throne, the place of eternal worship, the domain of the

Kingdom, the glory of God's presence. Of course, we are always in the presence of God, but we acknowledge an intensification of that presence during worship. Jesus promised, "Where two or three come together in my name, there am I with them" (Matthew 18:20). For this reason, we must pay careful attention to the content and structure of the external process that orders the internal experience of coming into God's presence.

The Content of the Gathering

Throughout history, the Gathering acts have changed periodically, yet they have always been characterized by the simplicity of entering into God's presence. The act of coming before God is not derived from human intent, but from divine mandate. The worshiping community does not order or manipulate God's presence; rather, God calls us before the throne of heaven and bids us to journey into the dazzling light of the transcendent otherness; the *mysterium tremendum*. Here the worshiping community acknowledges the transcendent otherness of the Holy God who is surrounded by the heavenly host of beings who forever sing the praise of God. It is then and only then that the assembled body joins the heavenly throng to burst forth into acts of praise such as the Gloria in Excelsis Deo, the Te Deum, or other words and songs that befit the Triune majesty of the one who alone is named God.

In God's presence the worshiper sees himself or herself against the dazzling and impenetrable light as a dependent creature, a rebellious son or daughter of the Creator, a wounded, broken, sinful human being. The only adequate response is one of humble confession of what it means to be a creature in rebellion against the Almighty, after which God speaks comforting words of forgiveness and healing to the listening heart. Once these actions have taken place, an opening prayer provides an appropriate transition from the Gathering to the hearing of the Word. (See table E.)

<u>TABLE E</u>: THE CONTENT AND STRUCTURE OF THE GATHERING

THE PRESENCE OF GOD IN THE ETERNAL KINGDOM

To journey into God's presence generally follows the sequence above. Some churches will place the confession before the act of praise. In either case the goal of the Gathering is to come into God's presence through acts of worship that appropriately symbolize the spiritual movement of ascent into the heavens, the place of eternal worship.

The Structure of the Gathering

The key to planning the structure of the Gathering is found in the content of the Gathering itself. Structure or order is always the means by which the content is delivered; when this rule of thumb is kept in mind there are two general procedures to follow. The first is to choose those acts of worship that establish and maintain the flow of the threefold process of coming into God's presence: (1) offering acts of praise, (2) confessing one's sinful condition, and (3) hearing God's words of healing and forgiveness. Strongly resist all temptations to add announcements or other acts of worship that would break or alter the narrative nature of the heart's journey into the throne room of God. (See appendix I.)

Second, worship planners must keep in mind that the Gathering is a narrative, not a program. A program is a series of unstructured and unrelated acts of worship that appear without any apparent connection. A narrative Gathering is characterized by flow and purposefulness. The Gathering is taking people some place. The journey into the presence of God is the simple, yet profound and powerful, business of establishing a relationship with the terms of divine calling. (See table E.)

The Experience of the Worshiper in the Gathering

It is important to remember that the external order of the Gathering is the means by which the internal experience of the worshiper is ordered. While the interior experience of the worshiper cannot be controlled (because it is ultimately a matter of the heart's disposition toward the Almighty), the content and structure provides the appropriate background against which the inner-experience of the willing heart finds spiritual direction. Of course, the opposite also applies. If the Gathering is a mere program it may entertain or even bore the person and thus prevent the journey of the heart from taking place.

Finally, note that the journey into God's place of eternal glory bears an affinity to the narrative of a comedic drama characterized by exposition, conflict, and resolve. The exposition is accomplished in those acts that bring the community into God's presence; the conflict is the experience of God's transcendent and eternal holiness in the face of the worshiper's finite sinfulness; the resolve is hearing the good news of the comforting words. No one needs to announce that the conflict and resolve of the Gathering is taking place. It is better to leave it to the worshipers to understand for themselves, so that the mystery of the relationship with God will be received in the inner-spirits of the congregation.

The Style of the Gathering

Although there are historical rules for the content and structure of the Gathering, there are no fixed regulations for the Gathering's style. Style is always a matter of appropriateness to be determined by particular worshiping communities. Style can range from formal to informal, from hymns and written prayers to choruses and extemporaneous prayer, from the full sound of a pipe organ to the beat of a drum, and from an ornate cathedral to a simple house church.

To summarize, the external process of the Gathering is that of coming before God, being formed into a worshiping community, experiencing the transcendence of God, knowing we are sinners before God, confessing our sin, and hearing God's words of forgiveness. The internal experience that takes place through this process is the realization of who God is and who we are in God's eyes. Planners of worship need to carefully think through both the external and internal processes and continually reevaluate the results of the Gathering every week. In the following pages the process of the Gathering in traditional, contemporary, and blended worship settings is set forth to provide samples of the external ordering of coming into God's presence. A careful examination of these examples will provide a better understanding of planning the process of Gathering for your congregation.

The Gathering in Traditional Worship

The purpose of the Gathering in traditional worship is to bring the people before God and to form them into a worshiping community, to offer praise to the transcendent God, and to be prepared to hear the Word of God through confession and forgiveness. Here is an example of the general structure of the content:

TRADITIONAL GATHERING ACTS

Prelude

Entrance Hymn (with procession)

Greeting	Coming before God
	and being formed into a
Call to Worship	worshiping community

Invocation

Act of Praise	Experiencing
	transcendence

Confession and Forgiveness	Knowing who we are
	and hearing God's word
	of forgiveness

Opening Prayer	Transition to the Word

In traditional worship services, the function of the prelude is to give the congregation time for silent preparation; whereas, the entrance hymn begins the formal act of coming before God. In many traditional churches the entrance hymn is accompanied by a procession of ministers and choir with crosses and banners (and possibly incense) which express the great pageantry of entering into a meeting with God. When the hymn is sung with fervor and the procession is conducted wholeheartedly, an overwhelming sense of coming into the presence of God may be communicated.

When the worship leaders have found their places, a greeting, call to worship, and invocation are formal signs that the meeting with God has begun. Now that the people are in the presence of God, a more intense expression of worship occurs as the congregation sings an act of praise (most often Gloria in Excelsis Deo), which extols God and magnifies God's name. The congregation is now lifted into the very presence of God, the transcendent and Holy One. Here the people confess their sin. The minister then proclaims the comforting words of God's forgiveness and acceptance. When these opening acts of worship are acted out in thoughtful and intentional prayer, the worshiper is carried through the subjective experience of being brought into the very heavens and into the presence of God. In their acts of worship God ministers to the hearts of the worshipers and makes them open and vulnerable to hear the Word.

The Gathering music in a traditional or liturgical church is generally the organ prelude, the processional hymn, and the act of praise. Careful consideration is normally given to the mood of both the processional hymn and the act(s) of praise. The processional hymn is joyful, familiar, and capable of accompaniment with both organ and brass. Coming into the presence of God is a festive act, which if not expressed by the music, probably will not be experienced by the people. A hymn, as Augustine states, is "the praise of God in song." So convinced was he of this truth that he went on to say that the praise of God not sung is not a hymn.

The act of praise is addressed to God and extols God's worthiness of praise. The ancient Gloria in Excelsis Deo is the traditional act of praise. There are numerous musical settings for the Gloria, ranging from formal to folk or praise tunes. While the Gloria is really the most appropriate act of praise, other hymns or praise songs extolling God's worth can be used. Because the mood is one of joy and adoration, the musical expression should be fast and upbeat. In liturgical churches, the organist will literally let out all the stops on the Gloria. It is a song of great emotional content.

A canticle may also be sung in place of the Gloria, especially when sung to a metrical tune as in *The New Metrical Psalter.* In Christian worship a canticle is a song from the Bible apart from the book of Psalms. The most often sung canticles are the Benedicite, a song of Creation (from the Apocrypha); the Benedictus, the song of Zechariah (Luke 1:68-79); the Nunc Dimittis, the song of Simeon (Luke 2:29-32); and the Magnificat, the song of Mary (Luke 1:46-55). A good translation of these and other canticles can be found in *The Book of Common Prayer.*

An opening prayer brings closure to the Acts of Entrance and opens the way to the Service of the Word, in which the people will hear and respond to God, who now becomes present in the Word.

In traditional churches with a desire to blend the contemporary with the traditional, one of the following three things are done:

1. Some churches precede the prelude with a set of contemporary songs. These may be quiet prayer songs sung to the accompaniment of a guitar, a synthesizer, or a band (or sometimes still the organ).
2. Some churches add a set of praise songs immediately after the processional hymn. These songs should express an atmosphere of coming before God.
3. Some churches add a set of praise songs at the act of praise. If the Gloria in Excelsis Deo is sung, no other songs should be added.

Contemporary Gathering Acts

Contemporary worship is strikingly different from traditional worship, yet it seeks to do the very same thing: gather the people into the presence of God and prepare them to hear the Word of the Lord. Contemporary worship is also committed to the narrative nature of the Gathering. For example, the tabernacle model leads the worshiper through the gates and ultimately into the Holy of Holies. The shape of the Gathering in a contemporary worship setting may look like this:

CONTEMPORARY GATHERING ACTS

GATES ▐▌	➡	High praise Gathering songs.
OUTER COURT	➡	Songs about coming to worship. The experience of coming before God.
INNER COURT	➡	Songs about God. Here the transcendent nature of God is experienced.
HOLY OF HOLIES	➡	Songs of confession and relationship. Here the worshipers experience who they are before God and hear God's love and acceptance.

This congregational journey toward the Word is usually accomplished through praise and worship songs that are interlaced with appropriate admonitions from Scripture. (Such a type of Gathering is often referred to as music-driven.) For example, the congregation may begin with several songs that express the act of going through the gates. One popular song that expresses this idea is Leona Von Brethorst's "He Has Made Me Glad (I Will Enter His Gates)," which contains the lyrics, "I will enter His gates with thanksgiving in my heart, I will enter His courts with praise." The internal experience here is one of joy.

Once in the outer court, the congregation sings songs about coming to worship, such as "I Will Call upon the Lord" by Michael O'Shields and "Come and Worship" by Don Moen. These songs are usually robust and loud, accompanied by shouting and dancing. But once the worship leader admonishes the people to enter into the inner court, the mood becomes more reverent. Here the congregation sings songs about God such as "You Are the Mighty

King" by Eddie Espinosa or "We Will Glorify" by Twila Paris. Finally, the congregation becomes very reserved as the approach is made into the Holy of Holies. Now the people may assume a posture of humble kneeling, and perhaps some of the worshipers will be prostrate on the floor as songs are sung to God such as "I Love You, Lord" by Laurie Klein or "Father, I Adore You" by Terrye Coelho. These acts of Gathering may be closed with a prayer.

Contemporary worshiping communities that blend traditional substance into their narrative will do so through appropriately placed prayers and hymns. For example, the church may have a procession using banners, a Bible, and even a cross. Processions usually occur with the singing of a hymn that focuses on coming before God with praise. Contemporary churches also generally interlace the song sequence with an adaptation of prayers from the ancient tradition, particularly the call for purity and the confession of sin. By these Gathering acts the people are formed into a spiritual community. The experience is usually intense, accompanied by the raising of hands, the closing of the eyes, concentration on the presence of God, and a kind of spiritual abandonment. In these moments of quiet, meditative singing, the worshipers feel literally close to God and sense that God is ministering to their needs.

Blended Gathering Acts

Blended worship brings the traditional and contemporary together in creative ways. No universal pattern of blended Gathering has emerged, but below are three possible orders:

In blended worship the Gathering songs may take the place of the prelude and are sung as the people find their seats. After the Gathering song, a prelude may be played as a transition into the processional hymn. Then the entrance hymn (a classic hymn, not a chorus or gospel song) signals the movement into the presence of God, where the greeting, call to worship, and

BLENDED GATHERING ACTS

Example #1

Gathering Songs

Entrance Hymn with Procession   The experience of
coming before God

Greeting, Call to Worship,
and Invocation

Songs of Praise and Worship   The experience of
God's transcendence

Confession and Forgiveness   The experience of
God's forgiveness
and relationship

Opening Prayer   Transition to the
Word

invocation occur. In response to being in God's presence, the congregation bursts forth into the acts of praise. Here the congregation may be led in a set of praise songs drawn from traditional hymns, contemporary songs, or a blend of both. This time of praise may be followed by a confession as the worshipers stand in the presence of God. Closure to the Gathering and a transition to the Word may occur in the opening prayer.

In this second sample, worship begins with the biblical order of law and gospel. For example, the entire congregation may be kneeling or bowing in silent prayer. The ministers and choir may proceed halfway up the center aisle and then kneel in prayer. Together the minister and people proclaim a confession of sin. The confession may be followed by a proclamation of the word of forgiveness and a cue to worship. The congregation then stands and sings joyful

BLENDED GATHERING ACTS

Example #2

Silence	Experience the presence of God in the quiet
Confession and Forgiveness	The experience of knowing who we are and of hearing God's Word of forgiveness
Call to Worship Entrance Hymn with Procession	The experience of coming before God with a relationship already established
Acts of Praise	The experience of God's transcendence addressed by songs of praise
Opening Prayer	Transition to the Word

hymns about coming into the presence of God. Once the congregation stands before God's presence the people may burst forth in acts of praise that blend traditional and contemporary songs of praise. The praise time may end with a prayer that serves as a transition into the Service of the Word.

This third model blends the Gathering with the scripture readings. With joyful acts of entrance, the people are brought into the presence of God by the processional hymn, an invocation, and then the more solemn reading of the scripture. This is followed by the congregation standing and singing a set of praise songs and hymns in response to the Word of God. A unique feature of this model is that the Gathering and the Word are united in a

BLENDED GATHERING ACTS

Example #3

Silence

Processional Hymn   The experience of coming
before God

Call to Worship

Invocation

Reading of Scripture   The experience of hearing
    Old Testament   God's voice
    Psalm
    Epistle
    Gospel

Acts of Praise   The experience of God's
otherness and transcendence

Opening Prayer   A transition to the sermon may
contain words of confession
and forgiveness

single flow. Having the time of response after the scripture readings provides the congregation with the opportunity to respond to the Word of God. (See Table F for the place of music in the Gathering.)

Reflect on all of these various examples to structure the Gathering. Note how the content and the structure of traditional, contemporary, and blended worship are essentially the same; only the style differs significantly. Remember that the style is never the order of first priority in planning the Gathering. Start with the content, work to the structure, and end with the choice of style. (See table F.)

TABLE F: EXAMPLES OF THE FLOW OF THE GATHER-ING AND THE USE OF MUSIC IN TRADITIONAL, CONTEMPORARY, AND BLENDED SETTINGS

THE PROCESS	TRADITIONAL	CONTEMPO-RARY	BLENDED
1) Gathering; people are brought into the presence	• Organ Prelude • *Processional Hymn* • Greeting • Call to Worship • Invocation	• Band Prelude • *Set of Songs that accomplish the gatherings, interlaced with appropriate scripture, admonition, and prayers*	• *Gathering Songs* • Processional Hymn • Greeting • Call to Worship • Invocation
2) The Praise of God	• *Act of Praise* usually Gloria in Excelsis Deo	• *A Set of Praise Songs*	• *Hymn, Canticle, or Set of Choruses*
3) Relationship Established	• Confession • Forgiveness	• *A Set of Songs of Confession and Assurance*	• Confession • *Sung Response of Assurance*
4) Transition to the Word	• Opening Prayer (written)	• Opening Prayer (extemporaneous)	• Opening Prayer (written or extemporaneous)
COMMENTS	The Gathering in traditional worship is *word driven*	The Gathering in contemporary worship is *music driven*	The Gathering in blended worship is a *combination of word and song*

63

How the Acts of Gathering Are Changing

The previous section demonstrates various changing trends in the Gathering. Let us summarize how these acts of ascent into God's presence are being reshaped in many different churches. First, the acts of Gathering are changing from a program base to a narrative flow. I have already defined a program as a series of unrelated and unconnected acts strung together, which leaves the congregation with a sense of never moving from one place to the next. In the past a worship committee may have said, "Let's see, we need a hymn, a scripture, a prayer, and maybe something else to fit in between." This kind of thinking did not allow for movement, for journey, for narrative. A narrative, on the other hand, moves the people sequentially on an uninterrupted journey toward the presence of God. The acts of Gathering described above are characterized by a flow of worship that brings the people into an experience in the presence of God.

A second significant change taking place in Gathering is the focus on music. In many contemporary churches the acts of Gathering are carried out almost exclusively under the accompaniment of music. In addition, a wider variety of musical instruments has come to be utilized, including the guitar, the drums, and the synthesizer. While these instruments are used primarily in contemporary worshiping communities, their use in traditional churches is growing.

A third change is in the increased use of the arts, particularly in the procession. While processions have been used primarily in liturgical churches, they are increasingly being used in contemporary churches. Done properly, processions have the power to evoke deep emotional feelings as the congregation comes into the presence of God.

Finally, it is important to remember that the Gathering incorporates ministry. The primary ministry of the Gathering is that the world is put in order. This is particularly true in the acts of praise, the confession, and words of forgiveness. In praise God is acknowledged as the One who sits upon the throne. God rules both in heaven and upon earth. God is in control. In the congregational praise using either the Gloria in Excelsis Deo or a set of praise songs, the Triune God is enthroned, and we are put in our place as God's creatures. With praises and confessions, the true world order is proclaimed and our place in the world under God is affirmed.

Worship begins by gathering the people. The ritual of the Gathering is important because it establishes a tone of warmth and joy; it narrates the people into the presence of God; and it prepares them to hear the Word of the Lord. It is a spiritual journey into the presence of God, a movement toward the place where God speaks a decisive word into our lives.

Resources for the Gathering

The resources listed below follow the process of the Gathering presented in this chapter. These resources are equally applicable to planners of traditional, contemporary, or blended worship. Planners of worship in traditional churches may be able to use the prayer resources without significant changes. Planners in contemporary or blended worship may want to adapt the prayers for their particular worship setting. By taking time to study these resources you will be able to better understand the content that gathers the people. Also, remind yourself that variety in worship is not attained by changing the process from week to week; rather, variety occurs by selecting various hymns, songs, calls to worship, and other prayers that are in keeping with the season of the Christian year. All the prayer resources below are in the public domain and may be used without permission. The origin of most of the prayers is not known. You are free to further update or paraphrase these prayers. I have not attempted to be exhaustive, so you should consult other prayer books, particularly *The Book of Common Prayer, The United Methodist Book of Worship,* or *The Book of Common Worship.* All the following listed songs are in *Renew! Songs and Hymns for Blended Worship.*

A. Gathering Songs

Gathering songs may be sung while the congregation takes its place in the sanctuary. As the people enter they should be encouraged to automatically join the singing. For this reason, use songs that people know by heart.

HYMN EXAMPLES

"God Is Here!" by Fred Pratt Green
"God Himself Is with Us" by Gerhardt Tersteegen (eighteenth century)
"Cantemos al Señor" by Carlos Rosas
"Here in This Place" by Marty Haugen
"Come, Let Us with Our Lord Arise" by Charles Wesley
"King of the Nations" by Graham Kendrick
"Come and Rejoice" by Don Moen and Gerrit Gustafson
"The Gathering" by Ken Medema

CHORUS EXAMPLES

"We Bring the Sacrifice of Praise" by Kirk Dearman
"O, Come Let Us Adore Him" by J. F. Wade
"Come into His Presence" anonymous
"Lord, I Lift Your Name on High" by Rick Founds
"As We Gather" by Mike Fay and Tom Coomes
"As the Deer Pants for the Water" by Martin Nystrom
"Be Still and Know" anonymous
"In the Presence of Your People" by Brent Chambers

B. The Entrance Hymn

The entrance hymn signals the beginning of the formal acts of worship, particularly the procession and the entrance of the leaders of worship. Because the Entrance hymn offers the internal experience of coming into God's presence, it should be characterized by weight and substance. Below are several good examples for the entrance hymn:

"Praise to the Lord, the Almighty" by Joachim Neander
"Immortal, Invisible, God Only Wise" by Walter Chalmers Smith
"Alleluia! Sing to Jesus" by William C. Dix
"Holy, Holy, Holy! Lord God Almighty" by Reginald Heber
"Let All Things Now Living" by Katherine K. Davis
"Let the Whole Creation Cry" by Stopford A. Brooke
"Come, Christians, Join to Sing" by Christian H. Bateman
"Sing Praise to God Who Reigns Above" by Johann Schütz

Generally, choruses are not used for processions. They lack the weight and substance of the hymns. However, some contemporary songs are substantial enough to express the journey of coming into God's presence. Here are a few examples:

"The Lord Is Present" by Gail Cole
"Make Way" by Graham Kendrick
"Lift Your Heart to the Lord" by John E. Bowers
"Majesty" by Jack W. Hayford
"Great Are You, Lord" by Steve and Vikki Cook
"Hosanna" by Carl Tuttle
"Praise, I Will Praise You, Lord" by Claude Fraysse
"I Will Exalt My God, My King" by Casiodoro Cardenas
"I Sing Praises," by Terry MacAlmon

C. The Greeting

The greeting during worship is a Christian exchange between the worship leader and the people. After the procession and entrance hymn has been sung, the worship leader may turn to the people, stretch forth his or her arms, and offer a greeting to which the people respond. This greeting can be conducted in either a formal or informal manner.

TRADITIONAL FORMS OF GREETING

The LORD be with you.
And also with you. (Ruth 2:4)

or

The grace of our Lord Jesus Christ be with you all.
And also with you. (2 Thessalonians 3:18)
or

Grace and peace to you from God our Father and from the Lord Jesus Christ.
And also with you. (Romans 1:7)

Other passages of scripture that can be used as a greeting to the congregation: 2 Corinthians 13:14; 2 Peter 1:2; 2 Timothy 1:2; and Revelation 1:4-5

CONTEMPORARY FORMS OF THE GREETING

A greeting can often be prepared from the scripture texts of the day. The greeting works best when it is short and succinct. Take a phrase out of one of the scripture readings, and put it into a form of greeting, similar to the example below:

Leader: Brothers and sisters in Christ, today I greet you with the words of St. Paul, taken from today's Epistle reading, Ephesians 1:9: God has "made known to us the mystery of his will."

People: Thanks be to God.

D. The Call to Worship

A call to worship is an act that brings the worshiping community into being. The call expresses the act of being brought up into God's presence, and it forms within the worshipers' experience the sense of God's intense presence in the community. Worship sentences may be said in connection with gathering songs, or they may stand on their own as a verbal proclamation of the gathering of the people to worship. Sometimes, when Gathering choruses are sung, the choruses may be linked by connecting phrases. Worship leaders may want to memorize the statement rather than read it. The call to worship can also be presented with an overhead projector or with a slide.

L = Leader   P = People   T = Together

L: Glorify the Lord with me.

P: Let us exalt God's name together. (Psalm 34:3)

(This call to worship may be followed with "We Will Glorify" by Twila Paris.)

or

L: I will lift up mine eyes unto the hills,

P: where does my help come from?

L: My help comes from the Lord,

T: the Maker of heaven and earth. (Psalm 121:1-2)

(This call to worship may be followed by "A Song of Creation" sung to the tune of "O For a Thousand Tongues." See Christopher Webber, *A New Metrical Psalter* (New York: The Church Hymnal Corporation, 1986).

PREPARING A CALL TO WORSHIP

The Call to Worship may be written from contemporary sources, such as a familiar song or from the scriptures of the day, particularly the service psalm. When preparing your own Call to Worship, keep in mind the following guidelines:

69

Structure it with a call and a response.

Keep it brief so it functions as an acclamation, not an instruction.

For creativity, combine it with a hymn, song, or chorus.

A SUNG CALL TO WORSHIP

A choir or worship team may sing an invocation, or an invocation of God's presence may be sung by the entire congregation. Examples include:

"O Come, Let Us Adore Him" by J. F. Wade
"Come into His Presence" anonymous
"As We Gather" by Mike Fay and Tom Coomes
"Bless His Holy Name" by Andraé Crouch
"Be Still and Know That I Am God" anonymous
"Lift Up Your Heads" by Steven L. Fry

E. The Invocation (of Gathering Prayer)

The invocation calls upon God to be present to the worshiping community. It generally follows the Call to Worship and precedes the Act of Praise. Modify the following prayers to fit the style of your worship:

Almighty God, to whom all hearts are open, all desires known, and from whom no secrets are hid: Cleanse the thoughts of our hearts by the inspiration of your Holy Spirit, that we may perfectly love you, and worthily magnify your holy Name; through Christ our Lord. Amen. *(The Book of Common Prayer)*

or

Eternal and ever blessed God, we bow before your Divine Majesty, adoring you, the Lord of heaven and earth, of whom and to whom are all things, unto whom be glory forever and ever. Amen. (Adapted)

PREPARING AN INVOCATION

For those who wish to prepare an Invocation themselves, there are four simple steps to keep in mind:

Direction	Example
1. Begin with a salutation to God.	Almighty God,
2. Continue with a description of God in which some aspect of God's character or action is extolled.	To whom all hearts are open, all desires known, and from whom no secrets are hid:
3. Next comes the petition, the heart of the Invocation. The petition is often followed by a statement of the end or purpose of the petition.	Cleanse the thoughts of our hearts by the inspiration of your Holy Spirit, that we may perfectly love you, and worthily magnify your Name;
4. Conclude with an ascription of praise.	Through Christ our Lord.

Furthermore, it may be a good idea if prepared Invocations are taken from the day's scripture reading.

SUNG INVOCATION

The Invocation calls upon God, particularly the Holy Spirit, to take up residence within the worshiping community. Here is a list of songs to the Holy Spirit that may be used:

"Be Still, for the Spirit of the Lord" by Dave Evans
"Come, Holy Spirit" by Mark Foreman
"Creating Spirit, Holy Lord" *Veni, Creator Spiritus* (trans. Ralph Wright)
"God Himself Is with Us" by Gerhardt Tersteegen

71

"Spirit of the Living God" by Daniel Iverson
"Open Our Eyes, Lord" by Robert Cull
"Prepare the Way" the Taizé Community
"Spirit Song" by John Wimber

F. The Act of Praise

The Act of Praise recognizes God's transcendence. In order to preserve the narrative quality of coming into God's presence, sing the Act(s) of praise after the Invocation. The internal experience of the worshiper is to encounter the transcendence of God. View the Act of Praise in terms of the narrative process of worship. The Entrance hymn has brought the people into a face-to-face position with God; the Call to Worship has resulted in the congregation becoming a worshiping community; the Invocation has asked God to be uniquely present. Now, the Act of Praise is the proper response for those who stand before the Almighty God of the universe.

TRADITIONAL SUNG ACTS OF PRAISE

Gloria in Excelsis Deo
Te Deum

TRADITIONAL CANTICLES
(ESPECIALLY FOR SPOKEN ACTS OF PRAISE)

See *The Book of Common Prayer* (pp. 85-96):
  The Song of Moses *(Cantemus Domino)*)
  The First Song of Isaiah *(Ecce, Deus)*
  A Song of Creation *(Benedicite, omina opera Domini)*
  A Song of Praise *(Benedictus es, Domine)*
  A Song to the Lamb *(Dignus es)*
  The Song of the Redeemed *(Magna et mirabilia)*
  Glory to God *(Gloria in excelsis)*
  You are God *(Te Deum laudamus)*

TRADITIONAL HYMNS OF PRAISE

"All Hail the Power of Jesus' Name" by Edward Perronet
"Crown Him with Many Crowns" by Matthew Bridges
"Give to Our God Immortal Praise" by Isaac Watts
"Holy, Holy, Holy! Lord God Almighty" by Reginald Heber
"How Great Thou Art" by Stuart K. Hine
"I Sing the Mighty Power of God" by Isaac Watts
"Immortal, Invisible God Only Wise" by Walter Chalmers
   Smith
"O For a Thousand Tongues to Sing" by Charles Wesley

CHORUSES THAT SERVE AS ACTS OF PRAISE

"All Hail King Jesus" by Dave Moody
"Alleluia" by Jerry Sinclair
"Bless His Holy Name" by Andraé Crouch
"Psalm 103: Bless the Lord" the Taizé Community
"Blessing, Honor and Glory" by Geoff Bullock and David
   Reidy
"Glorify Your Name" by Donna Adkins
"My Tribute" by Andraé Crouch
"Glory to the Lamb" by Larry Dempsey

G. The Confession of Sin

Once the congregation has experienced God's transcendence, the appropriate response is a confession of sin (as
in Isaiah 6:1-17). The internal experience of knowing that
one is accepted before God ministers to the worshiper
and produces an assurance of his or her relationship to
God. Below are several examples of traditional prayers of
confession.

O Almighty God, Lord of heaven and earth, we confess that
we have sinned against you in thought, word, and deed.
Have mercy upon us, O Lord, have mercy upon us after your
great goodness; according to the multitude of your mercies

73

forgive our sins; wash us thoroughly from our wickedness, and cleanse us from our sins, for Jesus Christ's sake. Amen.

(Adapted from the 1928 *Book of Common Prayer*)

or

Leader: Let us confess sins against God and our neighbor.

Silence may be kept.

Leader and Congregation:

Most merciful God, we confess that we have sinned against you in thought, word, and deed, by what we have done, and by what we have left undone. We have not loved you with our whole heart; we have not loved our neighbors as ourselves. We are truly sorry and we humbly repent. For the sake of your Son Jesus Christ, have mercy on us and forgive us; that we may delight in your will, and walk in your ways, to the glory of your Name. Amen.

(The Book of Common Prayer)

or

Holy God
Holy and Mighty,
Holy and Immortal One,
Have mercy upon us.

TRADITIONAL HYMNS AND SONGS OF CONFESSION AND LAMENT

"Amazing Grace" by John Henry Newton
"Forgive Our Sins as We Forgive" by Rosamond Herklots
"Kyrie Eleison" an Eastern Orthodox liturgy
"Lord Have Mercy" by John Michael Talbot
"How Long, O Lord" from Psalm 13
"The City Is Alive, O God" by William W. Reid Jr.

CONTEMPORARY SONGS AND CHORUSES OF CONFESSION AND LAMENT

"Change My Heart, O God" by Eddie Espinosa
"Come, Let Us Reason" by Ken Medema
"Create in Me a Clean Heart O God" from Psalm 51:10-12
"Humble Thyself in the Sight of the Lord" from James 4:10
"Purify My Heart" by Jeff Nelson
"Soften My Heart" by Graham Kendrick

H. The Words of Forgiveness

After the corporate confession, the minister speaks the words of God's grace and pardon. The internal experience is that of knowing that God accepts us as we are, yet calls us to a more holy life. Below are some traditional examples:

Almighty God, the Father of our Lord Jesus Christ, who desires not the death of us sinners, but rather that we may turn from our wickedness, and live; you have given power and commandment to your Ministers, to declare and pronounce to your people, being penitent, the Absolution and Remission of their sins: you pardon and absolve all those that truly repent and unfeignedly believe your holy Gospel. Therefore, we ask you to grant us true repentance and your Holy Spirit, that those things may please you which we do at this present, and that the rest of our life hereafter may be pure and holy; so that at last we may come to your eternal joy; through Jesus Christ our Lord. Amen.

or

May the Almighty and merciful Lord grant unto you pardon and remission of all your sins, time for amendment of life, and the grace and comfort of the Holy Spirit. Amen.

or

Soul of Christ, sanctify me.
Body of Christ, save me.
Blood of Christ, refresh me.
Water from the side of Christ, wash me.

Passion of Christ, strengthen me.
O good Jesus, Hear me.
Within your wound hide me.
Suffer me not to be separated from you,
From the malicious enemy defend me.
In the hour of my death call me,
And bid me come to you,
That with your saints I may praise you
forever and ever. Amen.

HYMNS OF FORGIVENESS AND ASSURANCE

"Amazing Grace" by John Henry Newton
"O Christ, the Healer, We Have Come" by Fred Pratt Green
"And Can It Be That I Should Gain" by Charles Wesley
"Our Great Savior" by J. Wilbur Chapman
"Christ Beside Me" by James Quinn
"Creating Spirit, Holy Lord" *Veni, Creator Spiritus* (trans. Ralph Wright)
"Forgive Our Sins as We Forgive" by Rosamond Herklots

CONTEMPORARY SONGS AND CHORUSES OF ASSURANCE

"Freely, Freely" from Matthew 10:8*b*
"Come, Let Us Reason" by Ken Medema
"Be Still, for the Spirit of the Lord" by Dave Evans
"Sanctuary" by John Thompson and Randy Scruggs
"Purify My Heart" by Jeff Nelson
"Humble Thyself in the Sight of the Lord" from James 4:10

I. The Opening Prayer

The Opening Prayer brings an end to the Gathering and projects the theme of the season, year, and day (in the Christian calendar). It serves as a transition from the Gathering to the Service of the Word. (Opening prayers for every Sunday of the Christian year are located in resources such as *The Book of Common Prayer*, pp. 211-36.) When preparing opening prayers, the following form may be used as a guide:

Direction	Example
1. An address to God	O God,
2. A reference to one of God's divine attributes or saving actions	you have prepared for those who love you such good things as surpass our understanding:
3. A petition related to the day's theme or the position in the church's year—often with a clause describing the end or purpose of the petition	Pour into our hearts such love towards you, that we, loving you in all things and above all things, may obtain your promises, which exceed all that we can desire;
4. A concluding doxology	through Jesus Christ our Lord who lives and reigns with you and the Holy Spirit, one God, forever and ever. Amen. *(Book of Common Prayer)*

In some churches the Passing of the Peace is observed following the Gathering acts. The congregation has been lifted up into the presence of God, and having heard God's acceptance, worshipers are ready to pass the peace as a sign of reconciliation with God and with each other.

Guidelines for Planning the Gathering

The guidelines below present general principles for the Gathering and may be used with equal value by those who will plan traditional, contemporary, or blended worship services.

1. Your primary concern as the planner of the Gathering is to think through the content and structure and to pay attention to the worshiper's experience. The matter of style is a secondary concern that is dealt with after the desired content, structure, and experience have been thought through. Study the following pattern as a guide, and note the spiritual journey into God's presence, ordered by the acts of the Gathering.

Content and Structure	Worshipers' Experience
Gathering Acts Prelude, entrance hymn, greeting, call to worship, invocation	Worshipers experience the sense of coming before God and standing in God's presence in the heavens. The community is called upon to become a worshiping community (in the call to worship), and God's presence is invoked (the invocation). Here the worshiper needs to exercise his or her spiritual intention.
The Acts of Praise The Gloria in Excelsis Deo or a set of hymns songs, canticles, or choruses.	The experience of the transcendence of God is usually expressed in hymns or songs that extol God, particularly the Triune Godhead. Here the community of worshipers is brought into the very presence

of God in the heavens. The worshiper needs to express spiritual imagination.

Confession and Forgiveness
Historic prayers of confession with the words of forgiveness; biblical words of a song or chorus; or a time of silence followed by a corporate confession

The time of confession and forgiveness may be a special time of ministry during which the worshiper reflects on his or her sins and shortcomings and then hears the words of forgiveness and acceptance. The experience of the worshiper should be a sense of release accompanied by the feeling of joy.

The Opening Prayer
Use a written or extemporaneous prayer. The content shifts toward the theme of the service of the Word.

Having come before God and having heard the Word of forgiveness, the worshiper is now ready to hear God speak. The experience of the worshiper should be one of openness and vulnerability to the Word of God.

2. The process of the content, structure, and the worshiper's experience is a narrative (the content moves as a story with an inner cohesion)—not a program (a series of isolated and unconnected acts of worship appearing without connection). A program approach to worship is generally entertainment rather than a spiritual journey.

The structure of the content should have the appearance of an inverted V, representing an uninterrupted flow of the story of coming into God's presence and being made ready to hear the Word. For this reason, matters that interrupt the flow—such as announcements, missionary moments, the children's sermon, and so forth—should not appear during the Gathering. (For planning such elements, see appendix I. See also table E.)

3. Generally, it is not a good idea to introduce new songs during the Gathering. Gathering acts are analogous to acts of hospitality in the home. They are warm, hospitable, joyful, and characterized by brief greetings. Gathering acts build and establish relationship. If a new song is going to be introduced, teach it before the Gathering acts begin, so that the congregation will be comfortable with the song.

4. Remember the primary theme of the Gathering is, simply, to gather. Generally, planners do not thrust the theme of the Service of the Word into the Gathering acts. The opening hymn, the greeting, and the opening prayer may reflect the seasons of the Christian year, Advent, Christmas, Epiphany, Lent, Holy Week, Easter, and Pentecost.

5. The length of the Gathering will vary depending on the style of the Gathering and the age of the worshipers. In many churches the length of the Gathering has been extended to allow enough time for the process of the content to take effect in the worshipers' experience. Although standing is the usual posture for the Gathering acts, give permission for people to stand or sit. If the Gathering is long, the older members of the congrega-

tion may get uncomfortable. Permission to sit will allow them to experience the process without discomfort.

6. Now consider your style. Identify the choices that typically reflect your worship:

Traditional	Contemporary	Blended
Formal	Informal	A blend of the two
Word-driven	Music-driven	Combination of both
Organ	Piano, drums, guitar (band)	Blend of instrumentation
Hymnbook	Overhead system	Combination of both
Prayer book or bulletin	Worship leader or team	Combination of both
Procession	No procession	
Vestments	Informal dress	Formal or informal dress
Ten minutes	Thirty minutes	Twenty minutes
Written prayers	Extemporaneous prayers	Prepared prayers or free prayers

7. Evaluate a recent service of the Gathering in your church using the following questions. Use a separate piece of paper if you wish.

—Evaluate the content of the Gathering. How does it compare with the content set forth in Guideline #1?

—Evaluate the structure of the Gathering. How does it compare with the structure set forth in Guideline #1?

—Evaluate the experience of the worshiper ordered by your chosen content and structure. How does it compare with the experience of the worshiper set forth in Guideline #1?

—Were the content, structure, and worshiper's experience of your service characterized by a flow (as in the inverted V), or were they a program of unrelated acts?

—Was the theme primarily that of Gathering? Was it something else? Was it without purpose?

—Was the length appropriate to the desired outcome of helping the worshiper to center on the presence of the transcendent God and to prepare to hear the Word of the Lord?

—Was your style traditional, contemporary, or blended?

8. Prepare a Gathering for your church. The process of the content and structure has been placed in the left column. Place your acts of worship in the middle column and your expectations for the experience of the worshipers in the column on the right. Follow your style of choice.

Content and Structure	Acts of Worship	Worshipers' Experience
Acts of Gathering		
Acts of Praise		
Confession and Forgiveness		
Transition to the Word		

Chapter 3

The Word:
Hearing from God

*O Lord, heavenly Father, in whom is the fullness of light
and wisdom, enlighten our minds by your Holy Spirit and
give us grace to receive your Word with reverence and
humility, without which no one can understand your
truth. For Christ's sake. Amen.*

JOHN CALVIN

The Nature of the Word

The second part of the fourfold pattern of worship is
quite different from the Gathering. In the Service of the
Word, worship shifts from coming into the presence of God
to being and remaining in that presence. Worship has
moved from God's *foyer* into God's *living room*. The chief
action is communication: God speaks to us through the
Word, and then we respond.

The Content of the Service of the Word

During the worship service, the content of communication
between God and the worshiper is the Scriptures themselves.
Renewed worship brings something new to the Service of
the Word: it recovers the narrative basis that had been virtu-
ally lost over the past three hundred years. The Enlightenment was a time ruled by reason and the desire to achieve
truth by empirical methods. This "reign of reason" turned
the Bible into a series of propositions to be proved or
debunked; the scriptures were subjected to historical and
scientific criticism.

The effects of the Enlightenment on the Christian faith and way people viewed Scripture made a negative impact on worship. In conservative circles the Bible became a book that needed to be proved, or better, justified. Conservative seminaries sought to prove all the supernatural stories of the Bible using the tools of rationalism. These seminaries graduated students who walked into the pulpits of the world with the arguments for the faith. Consequently, the service of the Word was turned into a time of teaching, persuasion, and proof of the validity of the Bible.

In liberal circles the Bible became a book that needed to be reinterpreted. It was argued that the supernatural stories could not possibly be true, and liberals used the tools of reason and science to debunk the biblical narratives as myth. Nevertheless, they looked for a truth that stood behind the stories. Usually these were humanitarian truths or values by which people were to live "good" lives. Consequently, liberal preachers turned the biblical narrative into inspiring lessons for the growth of the human spirit.

In both cases, liberal and conservative, the *Story* was lost. By contrast, post–Enlightenment worship planners are learning from the Near Eastern cultures that point back to the origins of Scripture itself. The story of God's saving work in history was entrusted to a *storytelling* community. The people of Israel told and retold the stories of God working in their history, and these narratives were committed to writing. The entire Bible from beginning to the end tells how we were created in God's image, how we fell away into sin, and how God worked in history to restore our relationship. This story is the content of the Service of the Word. We recite the story; we proclaim the story; we sing the story; and we are called to live out the story. The heart and substance of the Service of the Word is the story itself!

With the recovery of the narrative base of the Bible, there is a return to the power of the story—to the message of redemption, salvation, and hope that is contained within all the stories of scripture. This content is the historical recitation spoken of in chapter 1: the content of the Service of the Word is unchanging. It is the story of God acting in history toward redeeming creation.

The Structure of the Service of the Word

Because the Service of the Word is essentially a proclamation of God's story, the structure of the Word is not a process or journey as is the Gathering; rather, it is a dialogue based on the theology of proclamation and response. It is an interchange between God and the worshiper, much like a living room conversation between the host and hostess and their guests. God speaks. The people respond.

The structure pictured below contains all the aspects of both proclamation and response developed over the centuries in the Service of the Word. Churches would normally not use all of these acts of worship in any given service. Keep in mind that these acts may be modified to suit the style of traditional, contemporary, or blended worship (see "the Style of the Service of the Word," p. 90).

Proclamation	Response
1. Old Testament reading	2. Psalm response (usually sung)
3. Epistle reading	4. An Alleluia (usually sung)
5. Gospel reading	6. Prayer or song of illumination
7. The Sermon (or homily)	8. An invitational, dedicatory song, creedal song, or talk-back sermon
	9. The prayers of the people (which may be preceded by a prayer song)
	10. The passing of the peace

85

In the earliest noncanonical description of worship by Justin Martyr in A.D. 150 we are told that, "The memoirs of the Apostles or the writings of the prophets are read as long as time permits. When the reader has finished, the president [that is, the minister] in a discourse urges and invites (us) to the imitation of these noble things" ("First Apology," trans. Cyril Richardson, in *Early Church Fathers*, Library of Christian Classics, vol. 1 [Philadelphia: Westminster, 1953], p. 287). During the first three centuries of the Church, several dozen individuals were crammed into small, house-church settings where the Scriptures were read with constant interaction and discussion. The picture of the early Church at worship is akin to people sitting around a rabbi and discussing a text. (Smaller churches may want to go back to the more informal reading-inquiry-conversation model of the early Church.)

Many of our churches today are too large for the informal setting of the very early Church. The structure above reflects the historical development of the Service of the Word since the time of the genesis of Christianity. It is a valid structure to stimulate our thinking about the form of the Service of the Word, and planners should feel free to use it creatively with their communication of scripture.

Music for the Service of the Word

Because the acts of worship shift from gathering into the presence of God to hearing God speak, the music should shift, from voices raised in praise to ears attentive to the Word of God as it is preached. This shift in mood should be toward a more meditative style that assists the congregation in hearing the Word. (See table G.)

Music of the Word can include:

1. The singing of the scripture lesson. Singing the scripture lesson was used in the synagogue and passed down to the early Church. Sung scripture is generally found only in the high liturgical church.

TABLE G: MUSIC IN THE SERVICE OF THE WORD

TRADITIONAL	CONTEMPORARY	BLENDED
• Old Testament Lesson • *Responsorial Psalm Sung* • Epistle Lesson • *The Alleluia!* • The Gospel Lesson • The Sermon • The Creed • Prayers of the People (may be sung) • Confession and Absolution • Passing of the Peace	• Scripture Reading(s) *followed by a Sung Psalm Chorus, an Alleluia, or both, depending on the number of readings* • Sermon set up Drama • Message • *Musical Response by solo or worship team* • Passing of the Peace	• Old Testament Reading • *Psalm sung—Traditional or Contemporary* • Epistle Lesson • *Alleluia!* Traditional or Contemporary • Gospel Reading • *Sung Prayer of Illumination* • Sermon • *Sung Response* • Prayers of the People • Passing of the Peace

The content and process of the Service of the Word is quite similar regardless of one's tradition. Variation occurs primarily in the style, especially the style of music. Music in any style follows the more meditative pattern that fits the mood of instruction.

2. Sung responses to the reading of scripture (generally with a psalm).

3. The singing of the Alleluia before the reading of the Gospel. This honors the reading and gives the congregation a proper sense of the import.

4. Singing an expression of faith. A response of faith may follow the sermon. Use the Nicene Creed, the Apostles' Creed, or a hymn of faith.

5. Singing a song of invitation or dedication. A response of

receiving or returning to the faith may be sung after the sermon.

6. Singing a prayer song before the prayers of the people.

7. Singing the prayers. Chant music best expresses the mood of prayer. Generally, chant prayer is only found in high liturgical churches.

It is appropriate to sing any of the above suggestions. For the most part, instrumentation for music in the Service of the Word should be used sparingly, and almost never when the singing is a form of chant.

The Experience of the Worshiper in the Service of the Word

The inward experience of the worshiper during the Service of the Word is captured by a conversation I had while on vacation in Michigan. I was asked, "What do you do?" When I replied that I was a professor of theology, an amused look spread over the questioner's face. He replied, "So am I." As we talked about our teaching experiences, the subject of scripture emerged. My new acquaintance made a statement I will never forget, "I want nothing more than that the Word of God will take up residence in my life and shape me into Christ's likeness."

Later, when I was reflecting on the meaning of the Word in worship, I thought of those words and realized that he had put his finger on what the Service of the Word is supposed to do in the worshiper's experience. God's Word takes up residence within us and shapes us into Christ's likeness. Unfortunately, in many churches the Service of the Word is often dull and lacks a power that can reach inside of us and change the condition of our hearts. This is due in part to the loss of a narrative-based proclaiming of the Word which we discussed earlier in this chapter.

The actual experience of the worshiper in the Service of the Word will vary from week to week. Experience is shaped by the service content, which changes according to the chosen Scriptures and the seasons of the Christian year. Nevertheless, one constant always addresses the worshiper in the Word: historical recitation. The preached Word always enters a particular, historical, cultural situation in the worshiper's life (just as it emerged from one). Consequently, one of the main requirements of the worshiper is to seek connections in God's Word from the past to the present.

How does the Word of God given to a community in the past break through into one's life *now*, accomplishing just as relevantly what the Word once fulfilled in the past? This will require attentiveness on the part of the worshiper, an ear and heart that aggressively seek to listen to what God has said and is saying. In order for the Word to take up residence within the person, it is furthermore necessary to hear with an intent or resolve. Resolve is the will by which we choose to let God inform and form our lives. When God speaks, we not only hear God, we also act on what we hear God saying and doing in our lives and in the life of the world.

The Style of the Service of the Word

The style of the Service of the Word will vary from church to church because style is always determined by what is appropriate for a particular congregation. A formal congregation may employ the same content and structure as an informal church. One church may read the scripture, another may dramatize the Word; one church may slightly alter a psalm, another may sing a praise chorus that draws on a psalm phrase; one minister may speak formally from the pulpit, reading the sermon, another may stand close to the people speaking in a colloquial manner; one church may recite the creed, another may engage in conversation about the sermon; one church may read formal prayers, another may ask members to pray publicly. There is no such thing as an established style that is right for all churches everywhere.

We turn now to an examination of the traditional, contemporary, and blended styles of the Service of the Word. We will see how each may draw on the same content, follow a similar structural pattern, and accomplish the same spiritual experience for the worshiper.

The Service of the Word in Traditional Worship

The structure of the Service of the Word in traditional churches follows the dialogical approach of the early Church. In traditional worship the scriptures are read, and responses are made to the reading with the Psalms. The sermon is normally followed by the Creed, the prayers of the people, and the passing of the peace. Below is a graph of the traditional model.

There are two things to note in particular about this historical and traditional pattern of the Service of the Word: the focus on the Word and the underlying structure. First, the traditional approach to the Word is to read four scriptures; recently this heavy emphasis on scripture reading has been recovered in the restoration of the lectionary, an organization of weekly scripture readings based on the pattern of the Christian year.

THE PRACTICE OF THE WORD IN TRADITIONAL, CONTEMPORARY, AND BLENDED WORSHIP

THE SERVICE OF THE WORD IN TRADITIONAL WORSHIP

90

Second, the structure of the historical Service of the Word is the twofold process of proclamation and response. God's Word is proclaimed and the people respond. The Service of the Word is dialogical in nature. For this reason, the congregation is constantly singing responses, saying the creed and the prayers, and passing the peace.

Some people complain that this traditional model of the Service of the Word is a model from the past. On the contrary, I have been in many traditional churches where the people express a great deal of liveliness in the readings and the responses to the Word, where there is good communication and heartfelt response. In these churches the traditional model is alive and communicates the Word in a powerful way.

The Service of the Word
in Contemporary Worship

In a contemporary Service of the Word the message is the dominant act of worship. Generally, the pastor takes a Scripture and teaches how it helps a person to live the Christian life in the world. Messages are often practical, inspirational, and challenging.

Contemporary churches will often conduct a drama to set up the message. Sometimes the message is followed by a solo or worship team song. The message of the song is usually one of commitment and dedication to Christ. Sometimes words of encouragement to receive Christ as Savior or to allow God to do some healing in one's life are offered up. The Service of the Word is usually concluded with a prayer. The graph below shows the structure of the Word in a contemporary church, a structure that follows the ancient pattern of proclamation and response.

A primary concern for most contemporary churches is to communicate the Word in such a way that the worshiper is challenged to make life-changing decisions. Consequently,

THE SERVICE OF THE WORD IN CONTEMPORARY WORSHIP

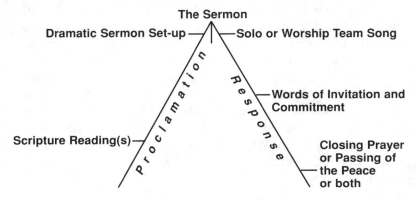

the strength of the contemporary Service of the Word is its immediate applicability for daily living. People often leave contemporary worship with a clear sense of what God wants them to do. This is one of the most significant reasons why so many contemporary churches draw such large membership. People want to hear what God asks of them and how God's way of life will bring meaning and stability to their lives.

The Service of the Word in Blended Worship

Although traditional worship is usually formal and contemporary worship is usually informal, blended worship may be either formal or informal. Like traditional and contemporary worship, blended worship follows the pattern of proclamation and response. Below are two models of the blended Service of the Word, one formal, one informal.

A unique feature of the Service of the Word in the blended model of worship is returning the Word to a more central place in the order of worship. For example, in most traditional, liturgical churches the Word is followed by the Eucharist, so the Word occupies the center. In most contemporary churches the Word is closed with

THE SERVICE OF THE WORD IN BLENDED WORSHIP

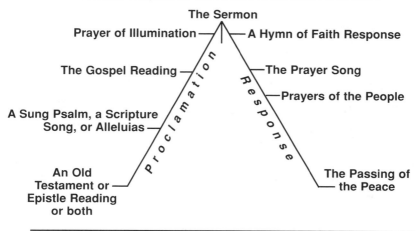

A FORMAL SERVICE OF THE WORD IN BLENDED WORSHIP:

The Sermon

Prayer of Illumination — A Hymn of Faith Response

The Gospel Reading — The Prayer Song

Prayers of the People

A Sung Psalm, a Scripture Song, or Alleluias

An Old Testament or Epistle Reading or both

The Passing of the Peace

Proclamation

Response

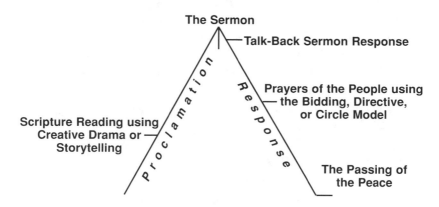

AN INFORMAL SERVICE OF THE WORD IN BLENDED WORSHIP:

The Sermon

Talk-Back Sermon Response

Prayers of the People using the Bidding, Directive, or Circle Model

Scripture Reading using Creative Drama or Storytelling

The Passing of the Peace

Proclamation

Response

prayer, and the service is ended. Blended worship generally follows the fourfold pattern, with either communion or the alternative time of thanksgiving being the principal response to the Word (see chapter 4). Conse-

quently, the pattern of worship in blended churches is as follows:

The distinct advantages of the fourfold pattern of worship will be detailed in chapters 4 and 5. It is sufficient to note here that the fourfold pattern provides not only a time for the worshiper to give special thanksgiving to God, but also a time in which God can uniquely minister to the needs of the worshiper (see table G).

It should be obvious that in worship the Word takes a central position. The reading and proclaiming of the Word is not an addendum to a time of singing, nor is it something that is ancillary to worship. It is the proclamation of the historical and present saving deeds of God, which can be experienced here and now as God delivers, liberates, heals, and relocates the lives of individuals, families, and communities. We gather to hear that saving and revolutionary Word. Because the Word is of utmost importance and crucial to the worshiper's spiritual health, we must explore the ways in which the Word can be communicated more effectively. The will to live a life in obedience to the Word proceeds out of a dynamic experience of the Word.

How the Service of the Word Is Changing

The communications revolution of the twentieth century has made a dramatic impact on the Service of the Word. The changes already begun during this century will only continue as churches become more sensitive to the need for better communication and greater levels of participation. These are the two central issues that must be faced by all worship planners if the Word is to pierce the heart and bring transformation to the life of the worshiper.

Achieving Better Communication

Both traditional and contemporary churches face the same problem of making the scriptures come alive. Clearly it is God who communicates through the Word, but often the human agent stands in the way of hearing the scriptures. It is therefore important that a church establish a lay readers group. The ministry of a lay readers group is to communicate the scripture clearly and effectively. Because scripture is an act of communication, those who engage in the ministry of reading should develop creative ways to communicate scripture. Reading and presenting scripture is the ministry of the laity. The reading of scripture by clergy was historically a clericalization of a lay ministry. Those churches that have returned scripture reading to the laity have been blessed to discover how creative the laity really are and how a more clear communication of the Word has added new depth to the Service of the Word.

Every church is blessed with good communicators who seldom get the opportunity to use their gifts. However, the lay readers group brings those gifted communicators together and provides them with the challenge of making the scriptures come alive. Here are four ways lay readers can communicate the scripture with power:

- Good reading
- Drama
- Storytelling
- Reading with an accompanying pantomime

Good reading is a must. Most of the time the scriptures will be read. Creative communication of scripture is more

95

occasional, particularly in traditional churches. Good reading derives from proper preparation. The most effective readers will prepare for their task in three ways. First, they pray the scripture that is to be read. They pray the scripture every day of the week as they slowly read it again and again with an ear toward what God has to say to them. Second, they study the passage and gain an understanding of its historical setting, the meaning of various words, and the theological ideas found within it. When they know the scripture in their minds and feel it in their hearts, their voices will express conviction, and the scripture will be heard with greater clarity and insight. Third, they practice the reading with other members of the lay readers group, hear the group's critique, and continually improve their skill. God desires the Word to take up residence in our hearts. We, the human vessels of God's voice, are to do all in our power to provide an open channel through which God can speak. This is the task of the lay readers group.

Presenting the Scripture through drama has made a comeback in the Church. In the fifteenth and sixteenth centuries, the Renaissance snatched drama from the Church and secularized it. In modern times the Church withdrew from the use of drama until recently. This return of drama has taken many forms. First, most liturgical churches will dramatize the Passion story on Palm Sunday and again on Good Friday. The Passion story is always read using readers for all the characters. The story reaches an emotional climax when the congregation, playing the part of the crowd, cries out, "Crucify him! Crucify him!" in answer to Pilate's question, "What shall I do with this man?"

Second, in contemporary churches a *sermon-setup drama* is often used. This drama is seldom from the Scriptures but generally captures a human situation as a prolegomenon to the sermon. I have witnessed some very engaging setup dramas on doubt, the question of prayer, where is God when it hurts, and other life-oriented issues.

Storytelling has also found a new place in the Church, particularly in the telling of the Gospel stories. Because the post-Enlightenment era has returned to stories, parables, analogies, and picture-formed thought as principal ways of communication, storytelling the Gospel account is a medium of communicating that has the potential to be highly effective. Some storytellers insist that the Gospel story be memorized word for word and quoted dramatically. Others allow the story to be told with interpretive liberties. For example, the storyteller who sees the story as an eyewitness within the story may feel free to develop the setting and provide imaginative insights into the story that are not included in the text (similar to what a preacher does during the sermon). The value of storytelling the Gospel is that the story comes alive, the actors appear as real people with whom twenty-first century people can identify. In most cases, the storytelling of the Gospel lesson will lead into the sermon; in exceptional cases the storytelling may be the sermon itself.

Another dramatic form of communicating the Scripture is reading with an accompanying pantomime. There are a number of biblical stories that lend themselves to being acted out as the reader reads the lesson. An acted-out lesson communicates the story visually and forms a picture that may make a lasting impression. For example, in one church I visited the Gospel lesson for the day was the raising of Lazarus. As the reader read the lesson and paused at appropriate places, the dancer who played the part of Lazarus moved from a condition of death to an exhilarating state of life and joy. Very few resources have been developed for lay readers groups who wish to do reading with pantomime movement, so Scripture presenters will need to rely on their own creativity when developing this kind of Scripture proclamation. Because dramatic presentation takes a great deal of time, most churches will use these forms of communication for special occasions, particularly for services around Christmas and Easter.

A final word needs to be said about the changing form of the sermon. While a plurality of approaches to preaching continues to dominate our pulpits, there is a major shift occurring in renewed worship. The shift is away from long pedagogical sermons and emotional evangelistic sermons to sermons that are a reflection of the Scripture texts of the day. A theme is drawn from the texts, and then commentary is made on how the texts speak relevantly to that theme.

Good communication is a key to good worship. Worship planners and evaluators will continually improve communication if they gather weekly to discuss, evaluate, and critique the communication of each service of worship. Worship is an act of communication in which God speaks and acts among us. For that reason every means by which communication can be improved needs to be pursued. Clear communication from God is necessary if the people are going to respond with their whole being. The key to a successful Service of the Word is an effective dialogue between God and the congregation.

Attaining Greater Participation

Methods of communication have shifted in society from objective forms that concentrate on logic and sequence to more subjective forms that focus on participatory immersion. In participatory immersion (consider the analogy of a sports arena), the participants shift from detached observation (the audience) to a state of personal involvement (the players). During worship, individuals are not to be spectators but players on the field. By becoming an active participant in the Christ Event, the worshiper's experience becomes radically charged.

This is not to suggest that the heart's response to the Word can or should be controlled or manipulated. An authentic, inward experience occurs when the worshiper brings to the communication of the Word the intent of the heart and a listening ear. One way of assisting the worshiper's heart is to provide an external form of response to God's Word, both read and spoken. During public worship this response needs to be corporate because it is the community responding together to the Word. Fortunately, the Holy Spirit uses the corporate response to get into the heart of each individual. A corporate response provides the opportunity for personal, heartfelt application of the Word.

There are nine types of corporate response that can be used during the Service of the Word, both to express the divine-human dialogue and to provide an opportunity for the heart's response:

- Response to the scripture reading
- Silence
- Responses between scripture readings
- The song of illumination
- The talk-back sermon
- The creed or alternative expression of faith
- The prayer song
- The prayers of the people
- The passing of the peace

First, the congregation may *respond to the reading.* In many churches, when the Word is read the people say nothing. They just sit passively as though what has just occurred is of little significance. We need to recover the sense that the reading of Scripture (and the sermon) is an in-breaking of God into our lives, a word of importance, a word of direction and counsel, a word that relocates us in God and sets the world in order. When the lay readers do what has been suggested above, the Word is given its rightful authority, and the people will be ready to respond. They will want and long to say their "Amen."

A form of response that has been used for centuries is as follows: at the end of the reading the reader proclaims with deep, heart-felt passion, "The Word of the Lord." The people respond enthusiastically, "Thanks be to God." Some churches will use a sung response such as "Thy Word is a Lamp unto My Feet." Traditional churches use a different response to the reading of the Gospel. At the beginning of the reading, the reader says, "The Holy Gospel of our Lord Jesus Christ according to (supply the Gospel)." The people then respond, "Glory to you, Lord Christ." At the end of the reading the reader says, "The Gospel of the Lord," and the people respond "Praise to you, Lord Christ."

A response can also be given at the end of the sermon. The minister may say "Amen" or "This is God's Word to you," and the people may respond, "Thanks be to God." Do not fear being creative with the responses to the Scripture reading and the sermon. Find a kind of response that is acceptable to your congregation. A response, whether said or sung, will heighten the emotional content of hearing God's Word, but take the time to instruct the people on why the response is crucial to good worship.

Second, an often neglected but very powerful response in worship is *silence*. Unfortunately, there are those today who speak of silence as "dead space." Silence is not dead space, but space that is alive with reverence. It reflects the admonition of Scripture, "Be still, and know that I am God" (Psalm 46:10). Silence allows the mind and heart time to create, to meditate, and to listen. Appropriate places for silence are immediately after each Scripture reading, after the message or sermon, and before prayer. A moment of silence before prayer is particularly important. The congregation needs time to center itself, corporately and individually. When the people become quiet before the Lord, the prayer will reach out and envelop them into its petition. It will become the prayer of the people.

Third, *a sung response* by the people may be placed between the Scripture readings. Many traditional churches have read the psalm for the day antiphonally because singing is a more powerful response than merely speaking. In a more traditional approach, the congregation may be led by a choir singing the verse, the people responding with a refrain. In a more contemporary church, the entire congregation may respond with a psalm or biblical chorus. When the worshiper has truly listened to the Word and then sings a biblical response with intention, the possibility of the Word being lodged in the person is heightened considerably.

Special preparation for the reading of the Gospel lesson is often practiced. For example, in the ancient Church the gospel book was carried in a procession while the community sang the Alleluias; then it was lifted up before it was read as a way of showing respect to the Word of God (a custom adapted from the synagogue). Today the Church needs to find new ways (or adopt old ways) to honor the gospel and point to its significance in the life of the community. How the Word is heralded is a matter of style and taste and may range from the more formal singing of the Alleluia in the traditional church to a drum roll in the contemporary church. Whatever the style, if appropriate to the congregation, it will communicate to the heart of the worshiper that this is no ordinary reading!

Fourth, preparation for an increased participation in the sermon can be achieved through *a sung prayer of illumination.* Prayers and songs of illumination are dedicated to the Holy Spirit. They invoke the presence of the Holy Spirit upon the preached Word and the heart of the worshiper. They call upon the Holy Spirit to open the heart and make it vulnerable to God's Word. The prayer or song of illumination is a very effective way to approach God's Word. It speaks of the transcendent mystery of the God who is wholly other.

Fifth, *the sermon* itself is also undergoing significant changes. The sermon originated in ancient Jewish traditions against the background of the synagogue service. A cursory reading of the book of Acts introduces us to the preaching content of Peter, Paul, and Stephen and clearly demonstrates that the Christian message was spread through the proclamation of preaching.

101

Following the New Testament period there were very few preachers and leaders of the stature of the apostles. Research into these centuries suggests that preaching in the villages and hamlets of the Roman Empire was not at all similar to what we understand as preaching today. A brief reconstruction of preaching in the first several centuries of the Church resembles the following: a layperson in the community would read a passage from Scripture, comment on it, then engage those assembled concerning the text and its impact on the Christian faith and life. Such a sermon was more akin to a group seminar then to the kind of sermon Christians are accustomed to today. These informal discussion groups probably continued into the fourth and fifth centuries, as the more organized method of the homily, or sermon, was being developed in the primary city-centers of faith (Rome and Alexandria). Once the more developed and expository approach to preaching became prominent, the conversational discussion groups from the rural areas died out, and preaching became the sole property of the trained preacher. Like prayer and singing, preaching was clericalized and taken away from the people.

To fully understand this historical development in preaching, we need to keep in mind the growth of the early Church and the corresponding shift in the worship setting. What began as small group meetings in house churches soon developed into thousands of people meeting in large basilicas, necessitating the organization and specialization of certain parts of the worship service. In small, intimate groups the conversational sermon fit well, but when the Church eventually became the official religion of the Roman Empire, most parts of the worship service, including the sermon, developed accordingly.

We are currently recognizing the distinction between communication in smaller churches and larger churches. The smaller church, like the early Church, is returning to a more conversational approach to the sermon while the larger church retains its theatrical approach to the sermon but seeks ways to get people involved in it. For example, small churches have special opportunities for intimate worship services. It makes little sense for a small church to pattern its worship after a large church. A smaller congregation automatically has the environment conducive to intimate singing, informal readings of the Scriptures, close prayers, and sermons that have a more direct and personal impact on those gathered. Imagine forty or so people sitting in a circle or facing each other in rows—that allows for conversation. Imagine the leader, an ordained person or called layperson, reading the Scripture and then simply, but powerfully, engaging in a conversation with his own friends and loved ones about the text.

In both smaller and larger churches today the *Talk-back Sermon* is being introduced as a way of getting people to respond to God's word. The minister will ask, "What did you hear, see, feel, or experience through the reading of Scripture and the sermon?" The people then turn to one another and respond. This kind of participation gets people involved in the spoken Word in more than an incidental way. It asks them how their lives can be transformed by the Word of God, which is the objective of the Service of the Word! Consequently, a response to the Word helps the worshiper to focus on his or her need for change and to make a resolve that results in spiritual growth and maturation.

While some of the suggestions proposed above may seem a little unorthodox, keep in mind this is so only because we have become thoroughly accustomed to the clericalization of the sermon. Those who may be threatened or put off by any of these ideas should remember that clericalized sermons were not the normal procedure for the early Church. It is also helpful to know that in the seventeenth and eighteenth centuries, Protestant worship sermons were almost always followed by congregational discussion. It was the custom for the minister to leave the pulpit following the sermon and to sit behind the communion table with the elders or deacons to discuss the sermon with various parishioners. This common practice was swept away by the introduction of revivalist worship during the nineteenth century.

Sixth, another kind of response to the sermon is *the saying or singing of the creed* or a creedal hymn or song. The creed most generally spoken in the Sunday service is the Nicene Creed, although some churches will use the Apostles' Creed. Both creeds are structured by the Trinitarian form, affirming what the Church believes concerning the Father, the Son, and the Holy Spirit. The creed itself is a telling of the story, a historical recitation that begins with God the Creator, moves to the work of salvation in Jesus Christ, and concludes with the present activity of the Holy Spirit. Unfortunately, the creed is often read as though it were an intellectual proposition of faith; whereas, the creed was originally meant to be proclaimed as a doxological burst of faith. Today many churches that use the Creed are doing so in a sung form because singing the faith expresses emotional content better than saying the faith.

Seventh, another method of attaining greater participation by the people is the use of *the prayer song* prior to the time of the intercessory prayers of the people. A prayer song is always quiet and meditative and forms the spirit of prayer within the worshiper. The heart gets in touch with God, allowing hidden needs to come forth to be presented to the Lord in the spirit of humility and dependence.

Next, *intercessory prayer* is also being revived in public worship. In most Protestant churches, people are familiar with the pastoral prayer; however, in the early Church, prayer was seen as the work of the people. The process whereby prayer was removed from full public worship and put into the hands of the clergy is one more way worship has been clericalized. At present, however, prayer is being returned to the people through the bidding prayer, the directed prayer, and the circle prayer. Returning prayer to the people is not only a means to attain participatory worship but, more important, a way of developing a praying people. When churches become full of people of prayer who learn how to pray openly in public, the life of prayer will be carried out of the sanctuary and made a daily habit of life. When prayer forms within the hearts of the worshipers, both inside the assembled body and outside in daily life, the worshipers' lives will be transformed from autonomous independence to the experience of continual dependence upon God.

Eighth, *the prayer of confession* is used by some churches following the intercessory prayers. This is particularly true of those churches that use a brief confession after the act of praise in the Gathering, such as "Lord have mercy, Christ have mercy, Lord have mercy." The argument is that in intercessory prayer we are brought before the very throne of God; is there a more appropriate place to confess our sin and hear the words of forgiveness? This is why the prayer of confession is often so close to the time of communion. In terms of the flow of worship, a prayer of confession is appropriate either in the Gathering (after the Acts of Praise) or in the Service of the Word (at the time of intercession). In either case, the worshiper is put into contact with his or her need and hears the good Word of God, the message of acceptance by God and welcome into God's presence.

Finally, *the passing of the peace* brings the Service of the Word to an end and prepares the people to enter into the time of communion, the giving of thanks for the death and Resurrection of Jesus Christ. The Passing of the Peace originated in the upper room with the first words of the resurrected Jesus to his disciples, "Peace be with you." Later both Peter and Paul reminded the Church to pass the peace when gathering together in worship. In his description of worship, Justin Martyr places the sign of peace at the end of the Service of the Word. It was the transitional act from the Word to the Table and expressed for the early Christians their relationship as brothers and sisters in the family of God. Consequently, it carried a confessional mandate: If you are not at peace with your neighbor, go get things right before you come to the Table.

In our culture we need to be more sensitive to new forms of communication that proclaim the Gospel story in ways that people understand. These nine classic forms of communication suggested for the Service of the Word open new possibilities and enable God's Word to take up further residence in the heart of the worshiper.

Resources for the Word

Forms to Introduce the Reading of Scripture (R = Reader, P = People)

Traditional Forms

Before the reading of an Old Testament or Epistle reading:

R: A Reading from _____

After the reading:

R: The Word of the Lord.
P: Thanks be to God.

Before the reading of the Gospel:

R: The Holy Gospel of our Lord Jesus Christ
   according to _____
P: Glory to you, Lord Christ.

After the reading of the Gospel:

R: The Gospel of the Lord.
P: Praise to you, Lord Christ.

Contemporary Forms

Before the reading:
A paragraph or two explaining the text is either read or said extemporaneously.

or

The hearer is asked to attend to the reading of Scripture with full attentiveness.

or

The hearer is asked to see a picture rather than to hear words.

After the Reading:
"May the Lord add a blessing to the reading of the Word."
The people respond, "Amen."

or

"May God cause the Word to take up residence in our lives."
The people may respond with a chorus such as "Thy Word Is a Lamp unto My Feet" or with words such as "All the Lord asks we will do."

Responsive Singing Between Readings

The Psalms are the most often used texts in the Service of the Word. The oldest form of music in the Christian Church is psalm singing, a form rooted in Hebrew worship. The earliest form of psalm singing is chant. The early Church developed metrical psalm-singing, and in 1719 Isaac Watts introduced a musical text for psalms in *The Psalms of David Imitate in the Language of the New Testament and Applied to the Christian State of Worship.* For example, "Jesus Shall Reign Where'er the Sun" is his rendition of Psalm 72, and "Joy to the World" comes from Psalm 98. In contemporary worship renewal, psalms have been recovered in all three styles—chant, metrical, and translation.

Although Protestants have seldom used chanting in worship, this musical form is currently undergoing a renaissance, especially as a means of prayer. Because chant is given to the repetition of a word or phrase, it is highly useful as a form of meditation, a way of centering in worship. Chanting the Psalms has the advantage of singing the actual text rather than a paraphrase of the text. Psalm chants are used primarily in the responsorial psalm during the Service of the Word, located between the Old Testament reading and the Epistle, and also in the gradual, the singing before the reading of the Gospel. In liturgical churches, the psalm is often sung by chant and not meter because the chant fits the mood of hearing the Word and concentrating on it better than meter does.

There are numerous chant patterns. One of the most widely used is the antiphonal chant. The soloist or a choir sings the psalm refrain or an Alleluia, then the congregation repeats it. The entire psalm is sung this way with the cantor chanting the verse and the congregation responding. This is a very beautiful way to sing a psalm and an effective one. Many contemporary choruses are also drawn from the Psalms and are appropriate responses to the Scripture reading.

Singing between the readings of the Scripture originated in the early Church, following the synagogue pattern of singing psalms. Today psalms and biblical songs may be sung by the choir and congregation (verse and refrain), or they may be sung in unison by all. Many choruses of the contemporary worship movement, which are based on the psalms or other biblical passages, may also be used as a response to Scripture readings. Examples include:

"How Majestic Is Your Name" by Michael W. Smith
"Sing to the Lord a New Song" by Hal H. Hopson
"A Shield About Me" by Donn Thomas and Charles
   Williams

"Hail to the Lord's Anointed" from Psalm 72, refrain by
   James Montgomery
"The Lord Is My Light" from Psalm 27, the Taizé Community
"Jonah's Song" by Edith Bajema
"Psalm 1: Planted by the Waters" by Patsy Hilton Kline

"Psalm 23: The King of Love" from Psalm 23

"Exodus 15:1, 2: I Will Sing unto the Lord" from Exodus 15

Singing the Gospel Alleluia

The high point of singing in the Service of the Word is the Alleluia sung before the reading of the Gospel. The word *alleluia* means "Praise Yahweh" or "Praise God." Many churches are restoring the honoring of the Gospel reading and are giving the Gospel reading its due place in worship. The recovery of the Alleluia adds a festive and celebratory character to the Service of the Word, which is otherwise quiet, instructive, and meditative. Today numerous Alleluias from all the cultures of the world are making their way into our worship. They are an important vehicle for communicating the emotional importance of Scripture.

A TRADITIONAL ALLELUIA

In traditional churches the Gospel acclamation is sung as the reader and acolytes process down the center aisle to read from "among the people." As the Gospel acclamation begins, the people stand. The Gospel acclamation is then sung in the following way:

1. The Alleluia is sung first by a cantor.
2. The Alleluia is then repeated by the congregation and choir.
3. The verse is sung by the cantor.
4. The Alleluia is repeated by the congregation and choir.

Example of the Liturgical Gospel Acclamation:

Cantor: Alleluia, Alleluia, Alleluia.
Congregation: *[Repeats the Alleluia.]*
Cantor: *[Sings verse or verses of the psalm.]*
Cantor and Congregation: *[Sing the Alleluia together.]*
(This sequence is repeated until the psalm is completed.)

A CONTEMPORARY GOSPEL ACCLAMATION

In nonliturgical churches the ancient Gospel acclamation may be replaced by a more contemporary song, such as a psalm, a canticle, a praise-tradition song, or especially the

Alleluia. The purpose of the song is to adorn the reading of the Gospel.

Examples of Contemporary Alleluias

"Alleluia" by Jerry Sinclair
"Alleluia" by Jacques Berthier
"Heleluyan" traditional Creek Indian song
"Halle, Halle, Hallelujah" traditional Caribbean song

Prayer Before the Sermon

A BIBLICAL EXAMPLE OF THE PRAYER BEFORE THE SERMON

Let the words of our mouths and the meditations of our hearts be acceptable in your sight, O Lord, our strength and our redeemer. Amen.

or

In the name of the Father, the Son, and the Holy Spirit. Amen.

TRADITIONAL EXAMPLES OF THE PRAYER BEFORE THE SERMON

O Master,
Illumine our hearts with the pure light of divine knowledge;
Open the eyes of our mind to understand your gospel;
implant in us the fear of your blessed commandments;
and trample down all our worldly desires:
That we may live in the Spirit,
Thanking you and doing the things that please you
For you are doing the things that please you
And unto you we ascribe all glory,
For you live forever with the Father
Who is everlasting and with the Holy Spirit
Who is all-holy and the giver of life.
Now and forever and unto ages of ages. Amen.
(Adapted from the *Liturgy of Saint John Chrysostom*)

or

Blessed Lord, who caused all holy Scriptures to be written for our learning: Grant us so to hear them, read, mark, learn, and inwardly digest them, that we may embrace and ever hold fast the blessed hope of everlasting life, which you have given us in our Savior Jesus Christ; who lives and reigns with you and the Holy Spirit, one God, forever and ever. Amen. (*The Book of Common Prayer, 1928*)

GUIDELINES FOR PREPARING A PRAYER OF ILLUMINATION

Direction	Example
1. An ascription to God	Blessed Lord,
2. A description of God's work with reference to Scripture	who caused all holy Scripture to be written for our learning:
3. The petition	Grant us . . . that we may . . .
4. A closing doxology	who lives and reigns . . .

SONGS OF ILLUMINATION

In place of the prayer of illumination a congregation may sing a song praying for God's illumination of the Word. Here are several examples:

"Spirit of the Living God" by Daniel Iverson
"Open Our Eyes, Lord" by Robert Cull
"Prepare the Way" the Taizé Community
"Blessed Jesus, at Your Word" by Tobias Clausnitzer
"Thy Word" by Michael W. Smith and Amy Grant
"Holy Spirit, Mighty God" by Calvin Seerveld
"Speak, Lord, in the Stillness" by E. May Grimes
"O Word of God Incarnate" by William W. How

Scripture Readings

Scripture for the Service of the Word may be based on the lectionary or *Lectio Continua*. The word *lectionary* derives from the Latin word *lectus*, which means "something read." A lectionary is therefore a prescribed set of readings. The origins of the lectionary go all the way back to the tradition of the early Church, which itself followed the synagogue practice of having a set pattern of weekly readings for worship. The Church eventually developed its own lectionary using the Christian year as its organizing principle.

The structure of the Christian lectionary is very simple: (1) Scripture is organized into a three-year cycle of readings (known as years A, B, and C); (2) each set of Sunday readings has an Old Testament lesson, an Epistle, a Gospel, and a psalm. All four Scriptures reflect the theme of the day in the Christian year. The value of using the lectionary is that worship will follow the themes of the Christian year; planners may work far ahead, knowing the texts and the season of the Christian year. Worship will cover the whole range of God's revelation in the three-year cycle of readings.

Lectio Continua means to select readings continually from one book. For example, a pastor may read and preach from the book of Romans or from a Gospel until the themes of the book have been adequately expressed. The advantage of this method is that it provides the congregation with an ordered study into one of the Scripture books. If the minister clearly lays out the divisions of Scripture upon which the sermon will be based, planners will have the advantage of knowing the Scripture text and be able to plan accordingly.

Invitational and Dedication Songs

INVITATIONAL SONGS

An invitational song may be used after the sermon. Here are some examples:

"Just as I Am" by Charlotte Elliott
"Come, Ye Sinners, Poor and Needy" by Joseph Hart
"Obey My Voice" based on Jeremiah 7:23
"Change My Heart, O God" by Eddie Espinosa
"We Choose the Fear of the Lord" by Kirk Dearman
"Lord, I Want to Be a Christian" African American Spiritual
"O Lord, Your Tenderness" by Graham Kendrick
"Softly and Tenderly Jesus Is Calling" by Will L. Thompson

DEDICATION SONGS

A dedication song may also be used after the sermon. Here are some examples:

"The Servant Song" by Richard Gillard
"Here I Am, Lord" by Dan Schutte
"Take My Life That It May Be" by Frances R. Havergal
"Be Thou My Vision" traditional Irish Hymn
"I Want to Walk as a Child of the Light" by Kathleen Thomerson
"Bring Forth the Kingdom" by Marty Haugen
"Sent by the Lord" Cuban song, trans. Jorge Maldonado
"The Gift of Love" by Hal Hopson

The Creed in Worship as a Response of Faith

The Nicene Creed is traditionally used in Sunday worship. Many churches, however, also use the Apostles' Creed. The Creed is usually said as a response to the sermon and as an acclamation of the faith.

THE NICENE CREED

We believe in one God,
  the Father, Almighty,
  maker of heaven and earth,
  of all that is seen and unseen.
We believe in one Lord, Jesus Christ,
  the only Son of God,

eternally begotten of the Father,
God from God, Light from Light,
true God from true God,
begotten, not made,
of one Being with the Father.
Through him all things were made.
For us and for our salvation
   he came down from heaven:
by the power of the Holy Spirit
   he became incarnate from the Virgin Mary,
   and was made man.
For our sake he was crucified under Pilate;
   he suffered death and was buried.
   On the third day he rose again
      in accordance with the Scriptures;
   he ascended into heaven
      and is seated at the right hand of the Father.
He will come again in glory to judge the living and the dead,
   and his kingdom will have no end.
We believe in the Holy Spirit, the Lord, the giver of life,
   who proceeds from the Father [and the Son].
   With the Father and the Son he is worshiped and glorified.
   He has spoken through the Prophets.
We believe in one holy catholic and apostolic church.
We acknowledge one baptism for the forgiveness of sins.
We look for the resurrection of the dead,
   and the life of the world to come. Amen.
      (The Book of Common Prayer)

THE APOSTLES' CREED

I believe in God, the Father almighty,
   creator of heaven and earth.
I believe in Jesus Christ, his only Son, our Lord.
   He was conceived by the power of the Holy Spirit
      and born of the Virgin Mary.
   He suffered under Pontius Pilate,
      was crucified, died, and was buried.
   He descended to the dead.
   On the third day he rose again.

He ascended into heaven,
   and is seated at the right hand of the Father.
He will come again to judge the living and the dead.
I believe in the Holy Spirit,
   the holy catholic Church,
   the communion of saints,
   the forgiveness of sins,
   the resurrection of the body,
   and the life everlasting. Amen.
                    (The Book of Common Prayer)

CREEDAL SONGS

Generally, contemporary churches do not say creeds, but usually sing a kind of creedal song or chorus. Examples include:

"We Believe (in God the Father)" by Graham Kendrick
"We Believe in God Almighty" by David Mowbray
"Meekness and Majesty" by Graham Kendrick
"What a Mighty God" by Jack Schrader
"There Is One Lord" the Taizé community
"Every Eye Shall See" by William and Gloria Gaither
"All Heaven Declares" by Noel and Tricia Richards
"Christ Beside Me" by James Quinn
"Fairest Lord Jesus" *Münster Gesangbuch,* trans. Joseph
   August Seiss

The Talk-Back Sermon

FOR SMALLER CHURCHES

After completing the sermon the minister may sit in a chair in a place where he or she can be seen by all. The minister may then say, "What did God say to you through the Scripture and sermon today? Please stand and speak clearly so that all may hear." The people may then respond with brief statements. These personal responses should not be sermons directed at people but a witness to what has been heard and how that may be applied to their spiritual pilgrimage.

FOR LARGER CHURCHES

The minister may say, "Please turn to one another and briefly respond to the Word of God. What did you hear, see, feel, and experience from God's Word?" A transition to the next act of worship may occur through the use of a song or chorus.

The Prayer Song

Prayer songs may be sung as the congregation moves into the time of intercessory prayer. These songs elicit from the worshiper the quiet spirit of prayer characterized by humility and expectation.

"Surely the Presence of the Lord" by Lanny Wolfe
"If You Believe and I Believe" from Zimbabwe
"Stay with Me" from Matthew 26
"Stay Here" from Matthew 26, the Taizé community
"Let Us Pray to the Lord" a Byzantine chant
"Lord, Be Glorified" by Bob Kilpatrick
"O Lord Hear My Prayer" from Psalm 102:1, 2; the Taizé
    community
"Lord of All Hopefulness" by Jan Struther

The Prayers of the People

One of the ways worship is being returned to the people is through the prayers of the people. There are several forms of participatory prayers used in renewing worship, including the bidding prayer, the litany prayer, the directed prayer, and the circle prayer.

THE BIDDING PRAYER

In the bidding prayer the prayer leader introduces an area of prayer concern, and the congregation then prays the concerns of that particular area. This form of prayer has the advantage of eliciting congregational participation in prayer and has been used very successfully in congregations that have been taught to pray. Here is a form of bidding prayer.

Leader: Please stand together for the prayers of the people. I will announce topics of prayer and ask you to respond with short sentence prayers. Please end each prayer with the word "Lord" so that the congregation may respond, "Hear our prayer."

Let us pray for the church universal, for all its people, and especially for those who work and minister in the church.

People: *[Offered Prayers]*

Leader: Let us pray for the needs of the world, for those who lead the nations, and for this nation.

People: *[Offered Prayers]*

Leader: Let us pray for the poor, the needy, and the sick.

People: *[Offered Prayers]*

Leader: Let us pray for the needs and the work of this local church.

People: *[Offered Prayers]*

Leader: [May close with a prayer, a confession of sin, or the Lord's Prayer]

THE LITANY PRAYER

In liturgical churches today, the people's prayer has been revived through the recovery of the litany prayer. Below is an example from Episcopal worship:

L: Father, we pray for your holy catholic church.
P: That we all may be one.

117

L: Grant that every member of the Church may truly and humbly serve you.

P: That your Name may be glorified by all people.

L: We pray for all bishops, priests, and deacons;

P: That they may be faithful ministers of your Word and Sacraments.

L: We pray for all who govern and hold authority in the nations of the world;

P: That there may be justice and peace on the earth.

L: Give us grace to do your will in all that we undertake;

P: That our works may find favor in your sight.

L: Have compassion on those who suffer from any grief or trouble;

P: That they may be delivered from their distress.

L: Let us pray for our own needs and those of others. *Silence. The Leader concludes the prayer.*

(The Book of Common Prayer)

DIRECTED PRAYER

Another variation of participatory prayer is the directed prayer model. It is usually practiced in larger churches or in churches that also practice a ministry time during the prayers of the people. In directed prayer, the minister leads the people in an opening prayer and then begins to mention various areas of prayer focus. After mentioning the need, time is given for the congregation to pray silently or quietly about that specific need. The minister can then list another need or end the prayer by simply saying, "Lord, hear our prayer." This more quiet version of bidding prayer offers time for counsel and ministry to take place in the front of the church during the prayer time, where people can be anointed for healing by prayer team members who have gathered to support them.

THE CIRCLE PRAYER

The circle prayer is generally used in large congregations

to attain intimacy. The worship leader may say, "Please gather in a small circle of four to six people. Express your prayer needs and pray together." The end of the prayer time may be signaled by a chorus or song, usually with a prayer focus.

GETTING PEOPLE INVOLVED IN PRAYER

One way to get the entire congregation involved is to ask ahead of time a dozen or more people to prepare a short prayer based on their thought and devotion to a specific subject during the week. For example, one person could be given the topic of "the needs of the world." That person will choose one subject, perhaps racism, and will spend the week watching the news, reading newspapers and magazines, and reflecting even on their own experiences in order to prepare a brief prayer for the service. This approach can motivate the entire body and can turn the prayers of the people into true congregational prayer. A praying congregation is a key to worship renewal and is a powerful witness to those who seek a living God.

The Confession of Sin

The time of prayer is often ended with a corporate confession of sin, followed by the Words of Forgiveness.

LITURGICAL CONFESSION ENDING THE PRAYERS OF THE PEOPLE

L: We pray to you also for the forgiveness of our sins. *Silence may be kept.*

L and P: Have mercy on us, most merciful Father; in your compassion forgive us our sins, known and unknown, things done and left undone; and so uphold us by your Spirit that we may live and serve you in newness of life, to the honor and glory of your Name; through Jesus Christ our Lord. Amen.

The Celebrant concludes with an absolution or a suitable Collect. (Book of Common Prayer)

NONLITURGICAL CONFESSION FOLLOWING THE PRAYERS OF THE PEOPLE

The minister may say, "Let us confess our sin to Almighty God."

Silence may be kept or the minister may make Confession for all by proclaiming a list of sins, personal, institutional, and national. The minister may conclude with an extemporaneous prayer and proclamation of God's forgiveness.

CONFESSIONAL SONGS

Any one of the following confessional songs may be used in place of the confessional prayers:

"Create in Me a Clean Heart" Maranatha!Music
"Ah, Holy Jesus" by Johann Heermann
"Forgive Our Sins as We Forgive" by Rosamand Herklots
"Sanctuary" by John Thompson and Randy Scruggs
"If My People" Maranatha!Music
"Purify My Heart" by Jeff Nelson
"Humble Thyself in the Sight of the Lord" Maranatha!Music

SONGS OF ASSURANCE

Any of the following songs of assurance may be used in place of the prayer of absolution or comforting words:

"Amazing Grace" by John Henry Newton
"Come, Let Us Reason" by Ken Medema
"O Christ the Healer, We Have Come" by Fred Pratt Green
"Freely, Freely" from Matthew 10:8*b*
"And Can It Be That I Should Gain" by Charles Wesley
"Our Great Savior" by J. Wilbur Chapman

The Passing of the Peace

The passing of the peace concludes the response to the Word. The sign of peace is expressed by a handshake or a hug extended to other people in the congregation. The sign of peace symbolically speaks to the reconciliation Christ has made for us. This has become a joyful time, a time to greet each other with a feeling of love through a physical gesture. Encourage great freedom and hospitality in this action as a way of expressing and experiencing the warmth and love of the community of faith.

FORM FOR PASSING OF PEACE

The Peace of the Lord be always with you.

or

The Peace of Christ be with you.
And also with you.

or

As our Lord said to his disciples,
"Peace be with you."
And also with you.

These words are said first by the minister or worship leader; then as the people exchange the peace they say them to each other. These words suggest that this is not a simple greeting among friends, but it is a gift of God's own peace passed from one to another. It is occasionally worth taking time to reinforce the meaning of the peace as a special time of community bonding. The exchange of the peace occurs with a handshake, a hug, or a kiss.

Guidelines for Planning the Service of the Word

The planning guidelines below are general principles for the Service of the Word and may be used with equal value by those who plan traditional, contemporary, or blended worship. Your primary task in planning the Service of the Word is to think through its content and structure and pay attention to the worshiper's experience. The matter of style is a secondary question to deal with once your content and structure have been determined.

Guidelines to Enliven the
Service of the Word

Because the nature of the Service of the Word is instructive, more than any other part of worship it is subject to "cerebral overkill." The following guidelines will help a congregation break through the impasse of a passive, uninvolved approach to the Service of the Word. Work on these issues one by one, and after completing the cycle, continue to improve the Service of the Word by returning again to each issue.

- As the Service of the Word is planned, recognize that its pattern is proclamation and response.
- Introduce the reading of Scripture in such a way that people will be encouraged to listen attentively.
- Establish a form of response to the Scripture reading.
- Find new ways to communicate Scripture (drama, storytelling, and so forth).
- Increase the use of the Psalms, spoken or sung.
- Be lavish with the singing of the Alleluias.
- Include acclamations at appropriate places (such as, "Thanks be to God").
- Develop a conscious response to the sermon (talk-back sermon).
- Develop a form of prayer that returns prayer to the people (for example, bidding prayers).

- Find ways to enhance the text through the arts.
- Establish the passing of the peace as a joyous expression of reconciliation.

Content: Choosing Your Texts

Since the Word is central to the Service of the Word, begin by choosing your texts below. (You may want to consult a lectionary unless you are using the *Lectio Continua* approach to Scripture in the Service of the Word.)

LECTIONARY LECTIO CONTINUA (TEXTS)

Old Testament _____   _____

_____   _____

Psalm   _____   _____
Epistle   _____   _____

_____   _____

Gospel   _____   (Psalm or Scripture
                                        Song) _____

_____

Read and study the chosen scripture texts. In a word or phrase, write down the central theme of the Scriptures.

Structure: Determining Your Order

The structure of the Service of the Word is based on the dialogue of proclamation and response. In the space below, prepare the outline of the Service of the Word, showing the proclamation on the left, the response in the middle, and the expected experience of the congregation on the right.

PROCLAMATION   RESPONSE   EXPECTED EXPERIENCE

Style: Traditional, Contemporary, or Blended?

Comment on the style you wish to use for one or more of the following acts of worship by marking each act. All parts of the Service of the Word have been included, but you should comment on the style of only those acts of worship that will be used in the service being planned.

How should the lay reader group present Scripture?

- good reading
- drama
- sermon setup drama
- drama with pantomime
- storytell the Gospel

How will you ask the people to respond to Scripture reading?

- with "the Word of the Lord"
- song or chorus

If you use a psalm or scripture song, what style will you use?

- choir with the response by the people
- cantor with the response by the people
- chorus

If you use the prayer of illumination will it be spoken or sung?

If you have a response to the sermon, which will it be?
- invitation
- dedication
- creed
- hymn or song of faith
- talk-back sermon
- other

If you use the prayers of the people, which form will be used?

- bidding prayer
- litany prayer
- directed prayer
- prayer circle

If you use the passing of the peace, what style works best with your congregation?

- a brief greeting to those nearby
- an extended time of leaving the seats and greeting a number of people

Compare your proposed order for the Service of the Word with a previous order.

PREVIOUS SERVICE   PROPOSED SERVICE

_____   _____

_____   _____

_____   _____

_____   _____

_____   _____

_____   _____

_____   _____

Summary. Fill out the structure below with the order of your proposed Service of the Word.

PROCLAMATION   RESPONSE

_____   _____

_____   _____

_____   _____

_____   _____

_____   _____

Chapter 4

The Table:
Celebrating the Resurrection

Let all mortal flesh be silent
and stand with fear and trembling,
and meditate nothing earthly within itself:
for the King of Kings and Lord of Lords,
Christ our God
comes forward to be sacrificed,
and to be given for food to the faithful;
and the bands of angels go before him
with every power and dominion,
the many-eyed Cherubim,
and the six-winged Seraphim,
covering their faces
and crying aloud the hymn,
"Alleluia, Alleluia!"

                    THE CHERUBIC HYMN FROM THE ANCIENT EASTERN LITURGY

The Nature of Table Worship

The third part of the fourfold pattern of worship differs significantly from the Gathering and from the Service of the Word. Worship at the Table is the Church's response to the Word, the time of offering praise and thanksgiving to the Triune God. This extraordinary celebration represents a second ascent into the heavens, a deeper and more full experience of the numinous. For in the Eucharist we join heavenly worship, and with the angels, the archangels, the cherubim and the seraphim we sing and cry aloud the eternal song of God's praises. What happens during the Eucharist is nowhere more clearly depicted than in the preface to the Eucharist liturgy of the Eastern church, the Saint John Chrysostom liturgy (fourth century). In the following preface prayer we gain a brief but powerful insight into that eternal worship:

It is fitting and right to hymn you, to give you thanks, to worship you in all places of your dominion. For you are God, ineffable, inconceivable, invisible, incomprehensible, existing always and in the same way, you and your only-begotten Son and your Holy Spirit. You brought us out of not-being to being; and when we had fallen, you raised us up again; and did not cease to do everything until you had brought us up to heaven, and granted us the kingdom that is to come. For all these things we give thanks to you and to your only-begotten Son and to your Holy Spirit, for all that we know and do not know, your seen and unseen benefits that have come upon us. We give you thanks also for this ministry; vouchsafe to receive it from our hands, even though thousands of archangels and ten thousands of angels stand before you, cherubim and seraphim, with six wings and many eyes, flying on high singing the triumphal hymn (proclaiming, crying and saying) [*People:*] Holy, (holy, holy, Lord of Sabaoth; heaven and earth are full of your glory. Hosanna in the highest. Blessed is he who comes in the name of the Lord. Hosanna in the highest.) (R. C. D. Jasper and G. J. Cummings, *Prayers of the Eucharist: Early, Reformed, and Traditional* [New York: Oxford, 1980], p. 89)

The Content of Table Worship

While Eucharist worship praises the Father, remembers the work of the Son, and invokes the presence of the Holy Spirit, the heart of Eucharist worship is Christ-centered. As in the heavenly worship described in Revelation, Christ is the center of our praise:

. . . because you were slain, and with your blood your purchased men for God from every tribe and language and people and nation.

Worthy is the lamb, who was slain, to receive power and wealth and wisdom and strength and honor and glory and praise!

To him who sits on the throne and to the Lamb be praise and honor and glory and power, for ever and ever. (Revelation 5:9, 12, 13)

In the heavens there is a constant and eternal historical recitation of Christ's great victory over the power of evil and death. Christ is worthy of eternal worship because he rescued the created order from its bondage to the evil one and has redeemed and renewed it for God. There are four images in the New Testament that speak to God's redemption of creation through Jesus Christ. These images provide us with the key to understanding the content of our worship at the Table: the breaking of the bread (Acts 2:42); the Lord's Supper (1 Corinthians 11:20); Communion (1 Corinthians 10:16) and Eucharist (1 Corinthians 14:16). An examination of these picture words will open the fullness of Table worship for us.

The meaning of *the breaking of the bread* is first expressed in the Emmaus road experience (Luke 24). Cleopas and his companion (probably his wife) were on their way from Jerusalem to their hometown the Sunday after Jesus' crucifixion. Jesus appeared to them as they traveled and accompanied them. As they walked, Christ drew from the Scriptures explanations that not only answered their questions but also touched their hearts. When they invited him into their home and set food on the table, everything changed. They suddenly recognized Jesus, the resurrected Jesus. When he broke the bread (a cultural ritual), the Bible proclaims, "Their eyes were opened and they recognized him" (verse 31). These two disciples then rushed back to Jerusalem to tell the other disciples that Jesus was alive after all, and their evidence was the recognition that had come "when he broke the bread" (verse 35).

Scholars agree that this text from Luke provides the key to understanding the experience of the early Christians during the breaking of the bread. Every time they engaged in this ritual the experience of the Emmaus road was, as it were, repeated. Jesus became known to those who participated in the breaking of the bread. Consequently, the breaking of the bread has always been associated with *the presence of the resurrected Christ.*

To find the origin of the next term, *the Lord's Supper,* we must jump ahead nearly three decades to A.D. 57, to the Greek city of Corinth. Apparently the Agape Feast (with its emphasis on the Resurrection) was still being practiced, but according to 1 Corinthians 11 it had got out of hand. Paul chided the Corinthians because at these feasts some of them were drinking too much and getting drunk (see verses 20-21). Paul suggested two things: eat your meals at home (verse 34), and share bread and the cup "in remembrance" of Christ (verses 24-26). Paul separated the symbols of bread and wine from the meal and shifted the focus from Jesus' Resurrection to his death. Consequently, Paul's corrective linked the Lord's Supper more strongly with sobriety than with the joy of the Resurrection—though this rite still speaks of both the death and Resurrection.

The third term that describes the experience of being at the Table with the Lord is also Paul's: "The cup of blessing which we bless, is it not the communion of the blood of Christ?" (1 Corinthians 10:16 KJV). Many biblical scholars see a reference in this term to a covenant meal, some versions using the word *participation* in place of *communion.* The bread and wine represent the agreement God has made with us through Jesus Christ. His death and Resurrection are the promise of salvation. He has conquered the powers of evil; he has trampled down death. He will ultimately destroy all the powers of Satan.

This "meal," then, is a foretaste of the kingdom to come—a visible, tangible promise for the future heavenly banquet at which we will gather to celebrate his victory over sin and death. As we eat it, we are lifted through time and space into another sphere where we sit down at the Table and feast together at the banquet of God. There we celebrate with God and with other believers God's ultimate victory over evil. By eating we establish, repair, and transform relationships. Eating *together* signifies relationship and oneness and fulfillment. Thus, communion refers *to the intimate relationship we have with the resurrected Christ.*

The fourth term, *Eucharist,* means "to give thanks." Paul uses this word in 1 Corinthians 14:16, admonishing the Church to speak in a known language: "If you are praising God with your spirit, how can one who finds himself among those who do not understand say 'Amen' to your thanksgiving [Eucharist], since he does not know what you are saying?" Here we find the theme of gratefulness. The minister, who stands at the Table and, in essence, gives thanks, is offering *gratitude to God for the gift of salvation through Jesus Christ.*

What should be the content of Table worship? We remember the death (Lord's Supper); we celebrate the Resurrection (breaking of bread); we enter into intimate relationship with the resurrected Christ at his Table (communion); and we give thanks for the work of Christ (Eucharist). The focus is on the Christ Event: on the life, death, and Resurrection; on the victory over the powers and principalities; on the final victory at the end of history when those powers will be put away forever, when God's *Shalom* will eternally rest over the re-created order of all things.

In other words, the content of Table worship is the Gospel. In the prayers that are said, in the actions that are taken, in the bread that is eaten and the wine that is drunk, the historical recitation and symbolic reenactment of salvation history reaches its most intense climax. The congregation breaks into its most passionate offering of praise for the

saving and healing power of Jesus Christ that is fully realized in us by the Holy Spirit.

The Structure of Table Worship

The historical structure of Table worship is the means by
which the life-giving and life-changing content of God's
work for us in Christ is communicated. The right form will
deliver the content, but the wrong form skews the content,
muddies it, and consequently prevents the desired experience of the worshiper. In Table worship, as in all other acts
of worship, the medium is the message, yet the biblical and
early Church pattern of Table worship is still simple
enough to allow for great variety and creativity. Let us first
examine the form of Table worship before we look at its
flexible style.

The service of the Table originated at the Last Supper (see
Matthew 26:26-29) and consisted of seven parts, in which
Jesus:

1. took bread
2. blessed the bread
3. broke the bread
4. gave bread to his disciples
5. took a cup
6. gave thanks
7. gave the cup to his disciples

Over the course of time these seven actions were con-
densed into four. For example, Luke may have been aware of
these four actions of the Table when he wrote "he *took* bread,
gave thanks, broke it and began to *give* it to them" (Luke 24:30,
italics mine). In the ancient Church the universal action at the
Table was compressed into four rites over the bread and wine:

1. the taking
2. the blessing (over both bread and wine)

3. the breaking
4. the distribution (of both bread and wine)

As worship developed, each of these four parts of Table worship was expanded with a prayer, a response, and symbolic actions. In the medieval era these subparts of the Table service became excessively elaborate. The Reformers sought to return the worship of the Table to its more primitive simplicity, but in the process lost valuable elements. Today the Reformation concern for simplicity is retained, but a greater emphasis is now being placed on recovering the substance of Table worship that was developed in the first five centuries of the Church.

The renewal of Table worship is not merely the recovery of ancient forms for the sake of antiquity. Rather, because these forms of worship are unique in their biblical imagery, they contain a greater power to deliver the meaning of what is occurring. Consequently, the revised forms of the ancient Eucharist prayers currently used in renewal worship are significant because of their faithfulness to the biblical and historical tradition. As such, they deliver a more profound experience of the four symbols of the Table: the death, the Resurrection, intimate relationship with Christ, and the expression of thanksgiving. Let us briefly examine each of the four acts of Table worship so that we understand better how the form is crucial to the experience of the content.

The first act is taking. According to Justin Martyr's description of worship, following the prayers the "bread is *brought,* and wine and water." It is important to note that *bringing* is a primary act of Table worship. Today, many renewing churches are returning to the action of bringing the bread and wine into the congregation following the Service of the Word. This challenges the present practice of those churches that set the Table before worship begins. To bring forth the bread and the wine creates a sense of festivity. This procession of bread and wine engenders a powerful emotional impact on the spiritual journey of the worshiper. For example, in a recent service at Tyndale Theological Seminary, seven students carried the bread and wine in procession as the congregation sang the song "I Am the Bread of Life." As the verses were sung the students processed with the bread and wine at shoulder height, but when the congregation sang the chorus, "And I will raise you up, and I will raise you up, and I will raise you up on the next day," the students stopped the procession and raised the bread and wine high above their heads. During the last two verses the procession stood before the Table with their backs toward the congregation and continued the same pattern of raising the bread and the cup during the singing of the chorus. The procession, accompanied by a song of invitation to communion, shifted our spiritual emotions from the hearing of the Word to the importance that lies at the heart of Table worship.

The second part of the historical structure of Table worship is the *prayer of thanksgiving.* The prayer of thanksgiving is itself worthy of an entire book, but here we can do no more than sketch out its content and point to the emotional impact it makes on the worshiper's spiritual journey. The content of the prayer of thanksgiving is trinitarian. It praises and blesses the Father, remembers the work of the Son, and invokes the presence of the Holy Spirit. The origin of this threefold pattern of prayer lies in the Hebrew *berakhah* (blessing) prayer. The *berakhah* prayer is ordered around the threefold pattern of praise, commemoration, and petition. For example, a prayer may say "Blessed be God (praise), who brought us up out of Egypt (commemoration), bring us into the promised land (petition)." The emotional impact of the thanksgiving prayer is based on its threefold emphasis on relationship. We enter into relationship with the Father through praise, with the Son through thankful memory of his saving deeds, and with the Spirit through the arrival of the unique and intense divine presence.

The third act of Table worship is the *breaking of the bread,* which brings together historical recitation and symbolic reenactment. The words "This is my body, given for you" are the words of historical recitation, and when the bread is broken these words are attended by symbolic reenactment. In the drama of Table worship, the action of breaking the bread, followed by the lifting of the bread and the wine cup for all to see, brings Table worship to a structural climax and turning point. In the Anglican tradition these actions are augmented by the cry of the celebrant, "Alleluia! Christ our Passover is sacrificed for us!" The people respond, "Therefore let us keep the feast. Alleluia." These words, and the actions surrounding them, communicate that Table worship offers praise and thanksgiving and prepares the community to enter into a joyful experience of receiving bread and wine, the ingesting of tangible symbols of salvation into their stomachs and the blood streams of their lives. The response of the people to the breaking of the bread may be a Lamb of God song.

The fourth structural element of the Eucharist is accomplished through *songs of communion*. The moment people begin to come forward to receive the bread and wine the congregation breaks into united singing. The Table service is then concluded with a doxology prayer offered to the Triune God for the whole work of salvation.

The Experience of the Worshiper at the Service of the Table

The experience during Table worship will be formed by the content and structure of the Table experience. This is an experience quite different than the experience formed by the Gathering or the Service of the Word, for at the Table the worshiper enters into an intense personal relationship with God. At the Table the worshiper may explode in praise and thanksgiving and may experience the healing touch of the Holy Spirit.

In order to have an intense spiritual relationship with the Triune God, the worshiper needs to grow in his or her

135

awareness of the prayer of thanksgiving offered over bread and wine. This prayer, shaped by the doctrine of the Trinity, is the very stuff of Christianity—the belief that people can have a personal relationship with God. In human relationships we praise those whom we love, we thank them for the things they do for us, and we desire to be with them. The worshiper needs to have the same attitude concerning the Table and must make his or her prayer a relational expression to God. Intentional praise becomes not only the offering of the community, but an intense, passionate, and highly personal prayer of the worshiper. In and through this prayer a personal and inward encounter with God takes place.

An intense encounter with God's supernatural presence takes place in the receiving of bread and wine, but this experience has been terribly damaged by modern thinking. Enlightenment rationalism persuaded both liberals and conservatives that the bread and wine were empty symbols, memorials to trigger the mind toward the cross and the idea of sacrificial love. There was no divine encounter during the taking of the bread and wine; it was all human recall, human intent, human sentiment. Now, however, in the post–Enlightenment renewal of the supernatural, there is a new appreciation of the words of Justin Martyr, "For we do not receive these things as common bread or common drink; but as Jesus Christ our Saviour being incarnate by God's word took flesh and blood for our salvation, so also we have been taught that the food consecrated by the word of prayer which comes from him, from which our flesh and blood are nourished by transformation, is the flesh and blood of that incarnate Jesus" ("First Apology," trans. Richardson, p. 19). The new appreciation of the mystery of Christ's saving and healing presence at bread and wine is captured in Cyril of Jerusalem's speech to the catechumens who gathered to hear his lectures in the Church of the Holy Sepulchre in the fourth century:

After this, [*i.e. after the priest has said 'Holy things for holy people'*] you hear the cantor inviting you with sacred melody to participate in the holy mysteries, in these words: 'Taste and see that the Lord is good.' Do not trust your palate to form the judgment; trust unhesitating faith. For those who taste are not bidden to taste bread and wine, but the body and blood of Christ thus symbolized.

When you approach, therefore, do not come forward with wrists outstretched, or with fingers spread open. Make your left hand, as it were, a throne for the right, since it is about to receive a king; and hollow your palm, and receive the body of Christ, adding your 'Amen.' Then, after you have carefully hallowed your eyes by the touch of the holy body, partake of it. Take care to lose none of it . . .

After partaking of the body of Christ, approach the cup of his blood also. Do not stretch up your hands, but bow down and say, in a manner worthy of reverence, 'Amen'; and be sanctified by partaking also of Christ's blood. And while the moisture is still on your lips, touch them with your hands, and sanctify your eyes and forehead and the rest of your organs of sense. Then wait for the prayer, and give thanks to God who has counted you worthy of admission to those great mysteries. (Henry Bettenson, *Later Church Fathers* [New York: Oxford University Press, 1973], pp. 46-47)

The personal dimension of the Eucharist is also expressed in the communion song. The songs of communion are not songs of proclamation but songs of prayer that help the worshiper enter into an intense personal and intimate experience with Christ.

A third powerful and moving experience at the Table of the Lord may occur through the anointing of oil. During this procedure, the worshiper will experience both healing and empowerment. The Eucharist and the anointing of oil both become a celebration of that one life that overcame death. In the power of his or her own resurrected life, the worshiper finds healing and empowerment to walk boldly into the future, born anew by the power of Jesus Christ.

This brief excursion into the experience of the worshiper at the Table demonstrates that something is missing in the current way most churches celebrate the Table. The aim of worship renewal is to restore the true experience of the death, the Resurrection, the intimate relationship with God, and the giving of praise and thanksgiving for these things. Such a spiritual engagement will revolutionize our worship and result in new spiritual vigor that will empower the personal commitment of faith and organize the ministry of the community.

The Style of Worship at the Table

Style is not the primary issue of Table worship. When worship planners understand the content and structure of Table worship, the style of communion worship ought to be consistent with the various cultural or background particularities of each congregation. The same content and structure may shape a highly liturgical worship or a causal free-flowing worship, but matters of style are related to space, music, and the various forms of prayer. We turn now to look at how Table worship in traditional, contemporary, and blended styles can reflect the biblical and historical content and structure.

The Service of the Table in Traditional Worship

Liturgical and traditional churches are most likely to reflect the content and structure of historical Table worship. This will be particularly true of Catholic and mainline churches. While each of these denominations may vary slightly, a general example (it will be described in this chapter) may be found in *The Book of Common Prayer*. I have charted the prayer according to the order in *The Book of Common Prayer*. It demonstrates the method employed in most liturgical and traditional churches:

The offertory sentence, or **Ascription of Praise,** serves as a call to Table worship. Standing before the people, the minister may say, "Ascribe to the LORD the honor due his name; bring an offering and come into his courts" (Psalm 96:8). Having signaled this ascent into the presence of God, the minister will then walk behind the Table and prepare the Eucharist (various rituals are done, such as pouring wine and water into the chalice). Next the leader (L) stretches forth his or her hands, leads the people into the *Sursum Corda,* and calls upon the congregation (P) to lift their hearts up into heaven:

L: Lift up your hearts.

P: **We lift them to the Lord.**

L: Let us give thanks to the Lord our God.

P: **It is right to give him thanks and praise.**

The minister then prays a preface prayer directed to the Father. This prayer speaks of the joy of coming into God's heavenly presence and acknowledges that the worship now taking place is with the heavenly host. In renewed worship this prayer, together with the *Sanctus,* is often such a moving experience that a sudden spiritual silence may descend into the room of worship, and people will experience the fullness of God's presence in such a deep and penetrating way that they will be moved to tears and to kneeling or even lying prostrate on the floor. One Episcopal minister related that he feels the presence of God in such a mighty way that sometimes he literally grasps the Table in order to remain standing.

Here are the words of the preface prayer and Sanctus:

It is right, and a good and joyful thing, always and everywhere to give thanks to you, Father Almighty, Creator of heaven and earth.

Here a Proper Preface is sung or spoken on all Sundays, and other specific occasions as appointed.

Therefore we praise you, joining our voices with Angels and Archangels and with all the company of heaven, who for ever sing this hymn to proclaim the glory of your Name:

Celebrant and People:

Holy, holy, holy Lord, God of power and might,
heaven and earth are full of your glory.
Hosanna in the highest.
Blessed is he who comes in the name of the Lord.
Hosanna in the highest.

The people then kneel in the presence of God, and the prayer continues with the **Commemoration,** a thankful praise for the work of Christ. The content is a brief historical recitation, much like a creed but with the emotional content of a doxology:

Holy and gracious Father: In your infinite love you made us for yourself; and, when we had fallen into sin and become subject to evil and death, you, in your mercy sent Jesus Christ, your only and eternal Son, to share our human nature, to live and die as one of us, to reconcile us to you, the God and Father of all.

He stretched out his arms upon the cross, and offered himself, in obedience to your will, a perfect sacrifice for the whole world.

During these words the minister will stretch hands over the bread and the cup.

The prayer then shifts to the **Words of Institution,** the very words of Christ spoken on the night of the last supper:

On the night he was handed over to suffering and death, our Lord Jesus Christ took bread; and when he had given thanks to you, he broke it, and gave it to his disciples, and said, "Take, eat: This is my Body, which is given for you. Do this for the remembrance of me."
After supper he took the cup of wine; and when he had given thanks, he gave it to them, and said, "Drink this, all of you: This is my Blood of the new Covenant, which is shed for you and for many for the forgiveness of sins. Whenever you drink it, do this for the remembrance of me."

The minister then adds the words that call the people to the **Memorial Acclamation:** "Therefore, we proclaim the mystery of faith." The people respond heartily with a robust sound: "Christ has died. Christ has risen. Christ will come again."

The minister continues the prayer with the **Anamnesis** (remembrance) and **Oblation** (offering) in a voice that expresses great joy: "We celebrate the memorial of our redemption, O Father, in this sacrifice of praise and thanksgiving. Recalling his death, resurrection, and ascension, we offer you these gifts."

The prayer then flows without a break into the **Epiclesis** (invocation), which now calls for the sending of the Holy Spirit so that Christ may be received in faith.

> Sanctify them by your Holy Spirit to be for your people the Body and Blood of your Son, the holy food and drink of new and unending life in him. Sanctify us also that we may faithfully receive this holy Sacrament, and serve you in unity, constancy, and peace; and at the last day bring us with all your saints into the joy of your eternal kingdom.

> All this we ask through your Son Jesus Christ. By him, and with him, and in him, in the unity of the Holy Spirit all honor and glory is yours, Almighty Father, now and forever. Amen.

Because the people are now in the very presence of Christ, the minister calls upon them to offer prayer to God using the very prayer taught by Jesus. After The Lord's Prayer is spoken or sung, **the minister enacts the drama of the breaking of the bread.** The bread is held high for all to see and then broken. A moment of silence is kept as the minister lifts the bread and the cup high above his or her head so all can see. Then in a strong, proclaiming tone the minister cries, "Alleluia. Christ our Passover is sacrificed for us!" The people joyfully respond, "Therefore let us keep the feast. Alleluia." The minister, with the elements still lifted, declares in a strong voice, "The gifts of God for the People of God. Take them in remembrance that Christ died for you, and feed on him in your hearts by faith, with thanksgiving." The people kneel in silence as the minister is served and then gives the bread and wine to the other servers. As the bread is being distributed the minister says, "The Body of Christ, the bread of heaven." As each individual receives he or she will say, "Amen." As the cup is given the bearers say, "The blood of Christ, the cup of salvation." The response again is "Amen." Next, the choir comes forward to receive. After the choir has returned to their seats, the congregation then comes forward row by row to receive. During the receiving of the elements the congregation will sing communion songs.

Hymns and songs are generally selected from traditional communion hymns such as "Now My Tongue the Mystery Telling," "Let All Mortal Flesh Keep Silence," "Jesus Remembers Me," or "Eat This Bread." In many renewed churches the time of communion is also used for the laying on of hands and the anointing with oil. After receiving the bread and wine, communicants may go to a designated place to kneel and receive the anointing with prayer for their special needs. This time of ministry is one of intense relationship with God and results in many instances of renewed faith and commitment, the answering of prayer, and the manifest presence of God in the lives of the people.

After all have been served and prayed for, the minister leads the people in a joint, closing doxology. This prayer is usually said quietly yet with the sound of strength and resolve:

Eternal God, heavenly Father,
you have graciously accepted us as living members
of your Son our Savior Jesus Christ,
and you have fed us with spiritual food
in the Sacrament of his Body and Blood.
Send us now into the world in peace,
and grant us strength and courage
to love and serve you
with gladness and singleness of heart;
through Christ our Lord. Amen.

The people are now ready for the closing act of worship, the Dismissal. (For music in traditional Table worship, see Table H.) Table worship may follow this pattern:

Communion worship begins with a **Song of Invitation** such as "Hallelujah, My Father" (by Tim Cullen) or "Be Still

143

TABLE H: COMMUNION MUSIC

TRADITIONAL	CONTEMPORARY	BLENDED
• Ascription of Praise • *Sursum Corda* • Preface Prayer • *Sanctus* • Prayer of Thanks- giving • The Word of Institu- tion • *Acclamation* • The Remembrance • Invocation of the Spirit • *The Lord's Prayer* • *Breaking of the* *Bread* • *Lamb of God Song* • *Invitation to Receive* • *Communion* *Hymns* • *Post Communion* *Song* • Closing Doxological Prayer	• *Song of Invitation* *to Communion* • Exhortation and Examination of Conscience • Prayer of Thanks- giving • *Praise to the* *Father Song (Holy,* *Holy)* • *Thanks to the Son* *Song* • *Invocation of the* *Spirit Song* • The Words of Insti- tution • The Breaking of the Bread • *Lamb of* *God Song* • The Invitation to Receive • *Communion* *Choruses* • *Post Communion* *Song* • Closing Doxological Prayer	• Ascription of Praise • *Sursum Corda* • Preface Prayer • *Sanctus* • Prayer of Thanks- giving • The Word of Institu- tion • *Acclamation* • Invocation of the Spirit • *The Lord's Prayer* • Breaking of the Bread • *Lamb of* *God Song* • *Invitation to Receive* • *Communion* *Hymns and* *Choruses* • *Post Communion* *Song* • Closing Doxological Prayer

The chart above is designed to show the use of music in Table worship. Note that the content and structure of traditional, contemporary and blended worship are quite similar. The difference between the approaches is expressed in written prayer versus free prayer, hymns versus songs and choruses, and formal versus an informal approach to worship. The singing of Table worship serves the text, lifts up the congregation as in the *Sacutus*, gives the congregation an opportunity to proclaim the gospel as in the *Acclamation,* and expresses the object of praise in *The Lamb of God Song. The communion song* of all three traditions reflects the death, resurrection, and intimate relationship with Christ. *The Post Communion Song* is a burst of praise and thanksgiving.

THE SERVICE OF THE TABLE IN CONTEMPORARY WORSHIP

The Breaking of the Bread

The Words of Institution —   — The Invitation to Receive

The Prayer
of Thanksgiving
Interspersed —
with Songs

Reception with
— Communion Songs
and the Prayers of
Anointing

Exhortation or
Examination of —
Conscience

Songs
of Invitation —
to Communion

The Closing
— Doxological
Prayer

for the Spirit of the Lord" (by Dave Evans). During the singing
of the song, which may be repeated several times, the bread and
wine are brought by a family and set on the communion table.
This action is followed by the pastor's **exhortation,** or the **Examination of Conscience.** Emphasis will fall on the meaning of the
Table, usually based on Paul's instruction in 1 Corinthians 11:17-
34. The minister then begins an extemporaneous **prayer of
thanksgiving** directed toward the Father, the Son, and the Holy
Spirit. After the prayer to the Father, the congregation may sing
a contemporary *Sanctus* such as "Holy, Holy, Holy Is the Lord
of Hosts" (by Nolene Prince) or "Holy, Holy" (by Jimmy
Owens). The minister will continue the prayer of giving thanks

145

for the work of Jesus, after which the congregation may sing "Lamb of God" (by Twila Paris) or "O the Blood of Jesus" (Anonymous). The minister then prays for the coming of the Holy Spirit; this is followed by a song invoking the Holy Spirit, such as "Spirit of the Living God" (by Daniel Iverson).

Next come the **Words of Institution.** The minister will generally quote verbatim the words of Matthew 26:26-28. When the minister speaks the words, "This is my body," the bread is lifted, then broken. Then, at the words "This is my blood of the covenant, which is poured out for many for the forgiveness of sins," the cup is raised. Lifting the bread and the cup up over the head so that they can be seen, the minister uses **words of invitation,** such as "O Taste and See That the Lord is Good." The people respond with a song such as "There Is a Redeemer" (by Keith Green). The people then come forward to receive the bread and wine as the congregation sings songs related to Jesus, to salvation, and to the new life and healing. **Communion songs** are primarily of the chorus genre and may include songs like "Abba Father" (by Steve Fry), "To Him Who Sits on the Throne" (by Debbye Graafsma), or "Give Thanks with a Grateful Heart" (by Henry Smith). During communion in a contemporary church, time may be provided for **prayer ministry.** Ministry may be confined to an area near the front of the church, or clusters of people may gather in small groups with arms locked around each other. The time of communion closes with a song of exaltation and praise such as "He Is Exalted" (by Twila Paris).

The **reception of communion** during the singing and the ministries of prayer is a powerful experience of the presence of God. Contemporary charismatic churches testify to the experience of unusual signs and wonders, gifts of knowledge and wisdom, and prophecies during this part of the service. Other contemporary churches, particularly in the Pentecostal tradition, often sing and dance after communion for twenty or thirty minutes. I experienced this response to the Eucharist in Christ Church of Nashville, a

Pentecostal Church where more than 2,000 people danced, shouted, and rejoiced for more than an hour after the reception of communion. The people were charged with emotion and filled with an overflowing sense of exuberant joy. (For music in contemporary Table worship, see Table H.)

The Service of the Table in Blended Worship

Table worship in blended churches is generally less liturgical than the traditional church and less exuberant than the contemporary church. Nevertheless, renewed worship at the Table in blended churches follows the same content and structure as the liturgical and contemporary church. There are generally more stylistic differences among blended churches than one would find in liturgical or contemporary churches. Liturgical worship is generally shaped by the use of a prayer book, and contemporary worship is usually shaped by choruses. Blended churches will use a combination of written and free prayers and a collection of hymns and choruses. Note the diagram of blended style.

A blended church may begin communion with the **Ascription of Praise** or with a **Song (or Hymn) of Invitation,** such as "I Come with Joy" (by Brian Wren) or "Love Divine, All Loves Excelling" (by Charles Wesley). The minister will then bid the people to Table worship with the *Sursum Corda.* Since blended churches use written prayers sparingly, the minister will usually say an extemporaneous **prayer of thanksgiving** praising the Father. This portion of the prayer is concluded with a traditional or contemporary *Sanctus.* The free prayer of thanksgiving continues with a recitation of God's saving deeds and culminates with thanksgiving for the work of Christ. Frequently in blended settings the congregation responds with a spoken or sung **Memorial Acclamation.** The free prayer then calls upon the Holy Spirit to become present to the congregation. This portion of the prayer is concluded with the singing of **The Lord's Prayer** to the Malotte tune or a more contemporary rendering.

147

THE SERVICE OF THE TABLE IN
BLENDED WORSHIP

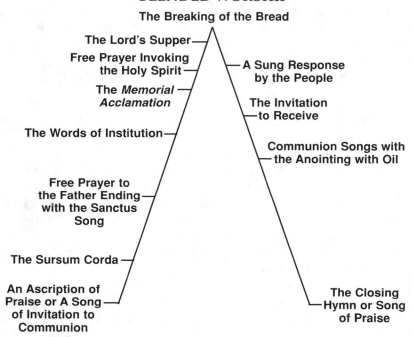

The Breaking of the Bread

The Lord's Supper

Free Prayer Invoking the Holy Spirit

A Sung Response by the People

The *Memorial Acclamation*

The Invitation to Receive

The Words of Institution

Communion Songs with the Anointing with Oil

Free Prayer to the Father Ending with the Sanctus Song

The Sursum Corda

An Ascription of Praise or A Song of Invitation to Communion

The Closing Hymn or Song of Praise

Blended Table worship now shifts from words and songs to words accompanied by powerful visual images of bread and wine. Blended worship tends to be extravagant with its symbols—a large loaf or loaves of bread with both the chalice and the cups (for people with preferences, wine is used in the chalice; grape juice in the cups). The loaf is now lifted and broken dramatically with the words, "Do this in remembrance of me." Then a pitcher containing the wine is lifted high enough for all to see, and the wine is poured into the large cup so that all can both see and hear. As this is taking place the minister proclaims, "Drink from it, all of you. This is my blood of the covenant, which is poured out for many for the forgiveness of sins." The people then respond with a song such as "This Is the Feast of Victory" (by John

W. Arthur) or "Eat This Bread" (by the Taizé Community). During the singing, the minister will partake, serve those who serve the bread and wine, and communicate the choir or worship team.

Once the choir or worship team has returned to their place they provide leadership for the **communion song.** Classic hymns and contemporary songs are often combined. The Crucifixion may be remembered through "Jesus Remember Me" (by the Taizé Community) or "Glory Be to Jesus" (translated by Edward Caswall). Music then moves to the symbol of the Resurrection with songs like "Gloria, Gloria" (by the Taizé community) or "He Is Lord" (from Philippians 2:9-11). The music then leads the worshipers, who have been brought through the Crucifixion and Resurrection, into a time of intimate relationship with Christ, with songs such as *"Ubi caritas et Amor* (Where Charity and Love Are Found)," a ninth-century song adapted by the Taizé community; *"O Christe Domine Jesu* (O Christ, Lord Jesus)," also by the Taizé community; "Healer of My Soul," by John Michael Talbot; or "Jesus, Stand Among Us," by Grahm Kendrick. During this time people receive the bread and wine, and those who wish receive the laying on of hands with an anointing of oil. After all have received, the congregation breaks forth in a closing act of sung praise, singing songs like "I Am the Bread of Life" (by Suzanne Toolan) or "Shine, Jesus, Shine" (by Graham Kendrick). The people may then kneel in silence as they reflect on the experience they have had with the risen Christ. The Table worship service is concluded with a **doxology prayer,** and the people prepare for the Dismissal. (For music in blended Table worship, see Table H.)

How the Service of the Table Is Changing

Recent scholarly studies regarding the practice of Table worship have made a considerable impact on contempo-

149

rary praxis. These studies have restored to Table worship the fullness of biblical content, its historical and theological shape, and the expression of joy and thanksgiving. Although these themes have already been mentioned in the previous sections of this chapter, a brief commentary on how scholarship is reshaping Table worship will help planners identify areas for change in their own worshiping community.

We may begin by noticing that renewed Table worship strives for a biblical fullness. I have already indicated that this fullness is recovered by allowing the content of Table worship to be formed by the four biblical terms: Lord's Supper (remembrance of the Crucifixion), the Breaking of Bread (a celebration of the Resurrection), Communion (intimate relationship and fellowship), and Eucharist (thanksgiving). In the past, churches frequently (and unfortunately) built their approach to the Table on only one of these four terms. They might think of themselves as a "Lord's Supper church" or a "Eucharist church." Recent scholarship has done much to dispel these stereotypes and now calls upon the Church to expand its understanding of the many dimensions of Divine encounter at the Table.

A second way Table worship is changing is in the pattern of its order and form. We now recognize that the form of Table worship in most Protestant churches originated as a reaction against Roman Catholic Table worship. Until quite recently, few Protestant churches ever used the word *Eucharist*. *Eucharist* was supposedly a Catholic word, a word to be avoided to show how Protestants differed from Catholics. Consequently, Protestant churches lost the full sense of *thankfulness* that is central to the structure of Table worship. (*Eucharist* means "thanksgiving.")

Protestants also made other changes to distance themselves from Catholics. They prepared the Table before worship and allowed the elements to remain visible (under a cover) throughout the Service of the Word. This change resulted in the loss of the dramatic act of bringing the bread and wine to the Table as an act of worship. Preparing the Table before worship also resulted in the confusion of symbols. During the Service of the Word, when the Scripture should have been the dominant symbol, the symbol of the Lord's Supper was obvious. On those Sundays when communion was observed, the theme of communion was mixed up into the Service of the Word. As communion themes and mediations began to dominate the Service of the Word, the fullness of both the Service of the Word and of the Table was lost. Protestants also introduced the practice of sitting passively in their pews as the bread and wine were passed down the aisles, losing the valued symbol of coming forward to receive.

The restoration of the biblical structure of bringing, blessing, breaking, and giving has resulted in a new Protestant shape of Table worship. Churches are now bringing the bread and wine in procession to the Table after the Service of the Word. This restores the flow of worship and puts the symbols of Word, bread, and wine in their proper places. Due to the research into the origins of the prayer of thanksgiving, the trinitarian structure is being revitalized: praise to the Father, thanksgiving to the Son, and the invocation of the presence of the Holy Spirit.

Furthermore, a new emphasis on the presence of the resurrected Christ experienced in the breaking of the bread has brought back the dramatic nature of the Table. The restoration of the act of coming forward to receive the elements has increased the participatory dimension of the Table. The introduction of the communion song has also played an important role in the recovery of joy at the Table. Many of the new communion songs, particularly those from the Taizé community, have provided new sounds of deep personal and joyful involvement in our relationship to Christ. These songs lift the spirit of the community into the heavenly mystery of the triumphant Christ and fill the people with joyful hope in a world that seems to be falling apart.

All of these rediscoveries have led to a new experience of the Eucharist, an experience that is restoring the original joy and the healing power of worship. As an evangelical pastor of a start-up church in Hot Springs, Arkansas, once told me, "My people would have it no other way. They literally explode with joy. It is the high point of our worship and our week."

Resources for Table Worship

A. The Ascription of Praise

The Ascription of Praise calls people to Table worship. One or more of the following Ascriptions may be used: .

Sacrifice thank offerings to God,
fulfill your vows to the Most High. (Psalm 50:14)

Ascribe to the LORD the glory due his name;
bring an offering and come into his courts. (Psalm 96:8)

If you are offering your gift at the altar and there remember that your brother has something against you, leave your gift there in front of the altar. First go and be reconciled to your brother; then come and offer your gift. (Matthew 5:23-24)

B. The Offertory Hymn (or Songs of Invitation to Communion)

The offertory hymn expresses the action of bringing bread and wine and of going forward to receive at the Table of the Lord. This hymn accompanies the procession of those who bring the bread and wine to the Table.

Examples of Traditional Offertory Hymns:

"I Come with Joy" by Brian Wren
"Love Divine, All Loves Excelling" by Charles Wesley
"This Is the Feast" by John W. Arthur
"Sing Alleluia to the Lord" an early Christian liturgy

Examples of Offertory Praise Music:

"Come, Let Us Eat" by Billema Kwillia
"Hallelujah, My Father" by Tim Cullen
"Be Still for the Spirit of the Lord" by Dave Evans

C. Preparation of the Table

Although the wine or grape juice is purchased at a store or through liturgical-supply vendors, many churches have appointed persons to bake the bread at home. Homemade bread adds a personal quality to the service. Several brands of nonalcoholic wine (such as St. Regis) are now available for those who want wine but avoid alcohol.

After the bread and wine have been placed on the table, the minister may lift the bread for all to see and say the following ancient Jewish prayer: "Blessed art thou, O Lord God, King of the Universe, who brings forth bread from the earth." The same may be done with the cup: "Blessed art thou, O Lord God, King Eternal, who createst the fruit of the vine."

D. The Examination of Conscience

If a prayer of confession has been made during the gathering acts or after the prayers of the people, it is not necessary to offer a prayer of confession at this point. If no prayer of confession has been made, or if an additional prayer of confession is suitable to the congregation, the following may be said:

The minister may say: "Hear the words of the apostle Paul: 'Examine yourselves, and only then eat of the bread and drink of the cup.'" (1 Corinthians 11:28 NRSV)

Here follows silence and extemporaneous prayer, or one of the following prayers said by minister and people together:

Father, Lord of heaven and earth,

153

I confess to you all hidden and open sins of my heart and
  mind, which I have committed until this day.
Wherefore I beg of you,
The merciful and righteous judge,
Forgiveness and grace to sin no more. Amen.
(Eastern Orthodox)

or

O Lord our God,
Our Creator and our Judge;
Proved every day, yet strong and patient;
Forgive we beseech you,
Our rebellion against your will.

When writing or preparing an examination of conscience,
observe the following structural guidelines:

DEFINITION	EXAMPLE
An ascription to God	Father,
A description of an attribute of God	Lord of heaven and earth,
The confession	I confess to you . . .
God's property of mercy	The merciful and righteous Judge,
The application of God's property	Forgiveness and grace to sin no more.

E. The Ancient Prayer of Thanksgiving

In the space below I have provided the earliest known,
full Eucharist prayer, attributed to Hippolytus in A.D. 215.
According to Hippolytus, this prayer was remembered
from his childhood, and he wrote it down as a guide for
prayer over the bread and wine—but only as a description, not a prescription. Note how the prayer praises the

Father, remembers the work of the Son, and invokes the presence of the Holy Spirit. Study this prayer for your own planning:

ORDER	TEXT	COMMENTARY
Dominus vobicum	The Lord be with you **and with your spirit.**	Praise to the Father
Sursum Corda	Lift up your hearts. **We have them with the Lord.** Let us give thanks to the Lord. **It is fitting and right.**	Worship ascends into heaven around the throne of God.
Preface Prayer	We render thanks to you, O God, through your beloved child Jesus Christ, whom in the last times you sent to us as savior and redeemer and angel of your will;	The preface to the prayer of thanksgiving and proclamation
Sanctus	(*Not found in Hippolytus*)	In the *Sanctus,* the Church joins with the angels and archangels in the heavenly song.
Prayer of Thanksgiving	. . . who is your inseparable Word, through whom you made all things, and in whom you are well pleased. You sent Him from heaven into the	The prayer of thanksgiving is is a recall of God's mighty acts in history, particularly God's act of sal- vation in Jesus

Virgin's womb; and conceived in the womb, he was made flesh and was manifested as your son being born of the Holy Spirit and the Virgin Fulfilling your will and gaining for you a holy people, he stretched out his hands when he should suffer, that he might release from suffering those who have believed in you. And when he was betrayed to voluntary suffering that he might destroy death, and break the bonds of the devil, and tread down hell, and shine upon the righteous, and fix the limit, and manifest the resurrection . . .

Christ. Note the creedal nature of the prayer as it recounts creation, incarnation, death, Resurrection, overthrow of evil and establishment of the Church.

Words of Institution

. . . he took bread and gave thanks to you, saying, "Take eat, this is my body which shall be broken for you." Likewise also the cup saying, "this is my blood, which is shed for you; when you do this you make my remembrance."

The repetition of the words of Jesus that lie at the heart of Table worship

Anamnesis

Remembering therefore his death and resur-

The word *anamnesis* means

	rection, we offer to you the bread and the cup giving you thanks because you have made us worthy to stand before you and minister to you.	"recall" and refers not to mental memory, but a Divine action in which Christ, the head of the Church, is remembered with the body.
Offering	And we ask that you send your Holy Spirit upon the offering of your holy Church,	The offering is the offering of the church's praise which ministers to God.
Epiclesis	that, gathering them into one, you would grant to all who partake of the holy things (to partake) for the fullness of the Holy Spirit for the confirmation of faith in truth . . .	The Holy Spirit is invoked so that those who partake may be confirmed in truth by the work of the Spirit.
Closing Doxology	. . . that we may praise and glorify you through whom be glory and honor to you, to the Father and the Son with the Holy Spirit, in your holy Church, both now and to the ages of ages. (Amen.)	The prayer ends with a Trinitarian doxology.

F. A Modern Adaptation of the Ancient Eucharist Prayer

The following prayer of thanksgiving is a modern adaptation of the ancient prayer of Hippolytus. Study its form

157

and content to understand the shape of the Eucharist prayer in worship renewal. Adapt the prayer to your local situation and style of worship. The various parts of the prayer are indicated in the comments on the right side of the page.

THE PRAYER OF THANKSGIVING	STRUCTURE AND COMMENTARY
The Lord be with you. **And also with you.** Lift up your hearts	*Sursum Corda*
	This ancient opening dialogue is now used universally.
We lift them to the Lord. Let us give God thanks and praise,	
Minister: It is right, and a good and joyful thing, always and everywhere to give thanks to you, Father Almighty, Creator of heaven and earth.	The Preface Prayer
Here the minister continues with a Preface Prayer suited to the particular occasion of worship. This prayer ends with words: And so, with your people of earth, and all the company of heaven, we praise your name, and join their unending hymn:	The content of the preface prayer is related to the Sunday in the church year or or to the theme of the celebration.
Minister and people sing or say:	*Sanctus*
Holy, holy, holy Lord, God of power and might,	The *Sanctus* has been set to many different tunes avail-

heaven and earth are full
of your glory.
Hosanna in the highest.
Blessed is he who comes
in the name of the Lord
Hosanna in the highest.

able in denominational
hymnbooks. Contemporary
churches may replace the
a traditional *Sanctus* with
with a contemporary
"Holy, Holy, Holy" (or a
stanza from a familiar
hymn).

*The people stand or kneel as
the minister continues with
the prayer:*

Commemoration

Holy and gracious Father:
In your infinite love you
made us for yourself;
and, when we had fallen
into sin and become
subject to evil and death,
you in your mercy sent
Jesus Christ, your only
and eternal Son, to share
our human nature, to live
and die as one of us, to
reconcile us to you, the
God and Father of all.
He stretched out his arms
upon the cross, and
offered himself, in
obedience to your will,
a perfect sacrifice for the
whole world.

Here, the saving events of
Christ are recalled.

*At the following words
concerning the bread, the
minister may hold it or lay a
hand upon it; and at the words
concerning the cup, to hold or
place a hand upon the cup
and any other vessel containing
wine to be consecrated:*

On the night he was handed over to suffering and death, our Lord Jesus Christ took bread; and when he had given thanks to you, he broke it, and gave it to his disciples, and said, "Take eat: This is my body, which is given for you. Do this for the remembrance of me."

After supper he took the cup of wine, and when he had given thanks, he gave it to them and said, "Drink this, all of you. This is my blood of the New Covenant, which is shed for you and for many for the forgiveness of sins. Whenever you drink it, do this for the remembrance of me."

Therefore we proclaim the mystery of faith:

Minister and people respond:
Christ has died.
Christ is risen.
Christ will come again.

The minister continues:

We celebrate the memorial of our redemption, O Father, in this sacrifice of praise and thanksgiving. Recalling his death, resurrection, and ascension, we offer you these gifts.

It is universally taught that a proper Communion cannot take place without the words of institution.

Memorial Acclamation
The memorial acclamation lets the people respond to the prayer of thanksgiving.

Anamnesis and Oblation

A prayer containing the remembrance and an offering of the gifts, as well as an offering of sacrifice and praise.

Sanctify them by your Holy Spirit to be for your people the body and blood of your Son, the holy food and drink of new and unending life in him. Sanctify us also that we may faithfully receive this Holy Sacrament, and serve you in unity, constancy and peace; and at the last day bring us with all your saints into the joy of your eternal kingdom. All this we ask through your Son Jesus Christ.

Minister and people:
By him, and with him, in the unity of the Holy Spirit all honor and glory are yours, Almighty Father, now and forever. Amen

And now, our Saviour Christ has taught us we are bold to say,
Here minister and people say or sing the Lord's Prayer.

The celebrant breaks the consecrated bread. A period of silence is kept. Then may be sung or said:

Epiclesis
A prayer invoking the Holy Spirit to be present with the people, confirming faith, and bringing healing to mind, body, and soul.

The Lord's Prayer

In the ancient church, prayers of intercession were often said at the end of the Eucharist prayer. Today the Lord's Prayer serves that place in Western worship. The bread broken and the outpoured cup are lifted for all to see, after which . . .

161

Alleluia. Christ our Passover is sacrificed for us; therefore let us keep the feast. Alleluia.

The Lamb of God song may be sung.

Facing the people, the Celebrant says the following Invitation:

The Invitation to Receive

The Gifts of God for the People of God. Take them in remembrance that Christ died for you, and feed on him in your hearts by faith, with thanksgiving.

The minister receives the Sacrament in both kinds, and then immediately delivers it to the people:

The Bread and the Cup are given to the communicants with these words:

The Words of Reception

The Body (Blood) of our Lord Jesus Christ keep you in everlasting life. Amen.

or with these words:

The Body of Christ, the bread of heaven.
The Blood of Christ, the cup of salvation.

During the ministry of Communion, hymns, psalms, or anthems may be sung.

The Closing Doxology Prayer

162

G. Sanctus Songs

In the Sanctus song the congregation joins the heavenly throng to sing the eternal song of God's praise, "Holy, Holy, Holy" (Revelation 4:8). Here are several examples:

"Holy Is the Lord" traditional, based on Isaiah 6:3
"Holy, Holy, Holy! Lord God Almighty" by Reginald Heber
"Holy, Holy, Holy Is the Lord of Hosts" by Nolene Prince
"Holy, Holy" by Jimmy Owens
"Holy, Holy, Holy Lord" by Jack Schrader
"Holy, Holy, Holy" by Bert Polman

H. Acclamation Songs

The acclamation song is a proclamation of the heart of the Gospel:

"Christ Has Died, Christ Is Risen" from an ancient liturgy
"Christ Has Died" *The Book of Common Prayer*
"We Remember His Death" *The Book of Common Prayer*
"Christ Has Died" by Marty Haugen
"The Threefold Truth" by Fred Pratt Green

I. The Lamb of God Songs

Lamb of God songs may be sung when the bread and wine are presented to the congregation:

"Lamb of God" by Twila Paris
"Jesus, Lamb of God" by Betty Pulkingham
"O Christ, the Lamb of God" by Joachim Decker

J. Invitation to Receive Communion

Call people to receive communion with any of the following acclamations:

O taste and see that the Lord is good.

or

This is the Lamb of God who takes away the sins of the world.
Happy are those who are called to his supper.

or

Lord, I am not worthy to receive you, but only say the word and I shall be healed.

K. The Communion Song

One of the most important features of worship renewal today is the recovery of the communion song. Communion songs are those that celebrate or recognize the Crucifixion, the Resurrection, the intimate relationship with Christ, and the thanksgiving for salvation in Christ. These songs shift communion from an overemphasis on Christ's death toward a celebration of the Resurrection.

The purpose of the communion song is threefold. First, it expresses the unity of the Church. This is not a time for instrumental music or choir anthems. It is a time for the whole congregation to join in unison. Second, the communion song organizes the spiritual experience of the congregation by ordering people's concentration on both the death and the Resurrection of Christ. The first several songs may dwell on the death of Christ; however, the majority of songs should express the joy of the Resurrection and the immediacy of the Spirit. Third, the communion song maintains a sense of the mystery of faith. Singing is a more powerful way to approach mystery than spoken words alone.

Some churches that have begun celebrating communion more regularly have opted to hold their extended times of praise until after their Table worship. Such an extended session at this part of the service emphasizes the joyous freedom and victory of the Christian due to Christ's victorious Crucifixion and Resurrection.

EXAMPLES OF COMMUNION SONGS

Traditional Hymns

"Gift of Finest Wheat" by Omer Westendorf
"Now the Silence, Then the Glory" by Jaroslav J. Vajda
"Let All Mortal Flesh Keep Silence" liturgy of Saint James
"Glory Be to Jesus" translated by Edward Caswall
"O Sacred Head, Now Wounded" by Bernard of Clairvaux
"When I Survey the Wondrous Cross" by Isaac Watts

Praise Tradition

"Broken for Me" by Janet Lunt
"O the Blood of Jesus" by Sister Delores Dufner, OSB
"Seekers of Your Heart" by Melodie and Dick Tunney and
   Beverly Darnall
"Soften My Heart" by Graham Kendrick
"I Will Change Your Name" by D. J. Butler
"Healer of My Soul" by John Michael Talbot
"*Ubi caritas et amor*" by Jacques Berthier
"Jesus Remember Me" the Taizé Community

L. The Rite of Healing

The Church has always practiced anointing with oil for healing. Renewed worship connects the rite of healing to Table worship. Renewing churches are increasingly using the time immediately after a person has received Communion for the laying on of hands and the anointing with oil.

A FORM FOR PRAYER OF HEALING

A person with the gift for the ministry of healing may stand at an appropriate place near the Table. After receiving the bread and wine, the one desiring prayer may present himself or herself to the minister. There is no need for an exchange of words. The minister lays hands upon the person who has come. Making the sign of the cross with oil on the communicant's forehead, the minister says, "I anoint you in the name of the Father, Son, and Holy Spirit." Then, clasping hands around the head, the minister may say, "May the Holy Spirit bring healing into your whole person, mind, body, soul, and spirit, and may you be filled with the presence of Christ."

Most charismatic and renewal churches are more comfortable practicing a thorough ministry of healing, which includes interview, anointing, prayer for guidance, and healing prayers. Teams that have been raised up in such churches can be stationed near the communion rail or at another appropriate place to offer such a healing ministry. As they leave the Table, communicants can receive in-depth help while not interfering with others who are partaking. If necessary, this ministry can continue even after communion and into the time of Dismissal.

M. Post-communion Song

The post-communion song is generally sung after all have received the bread and wine and the anointing of individuals with oil. The post-communion song is usually an outburst of thankful praise:

"He Is Exalted" by Twila Paris
"Hallelujah! We Sing Your Praises" a South African song
"Dona Nobis Pacem" traditional
"Dona Nobis Pacem Domine" by Jacques Berthier and the
  Taizé Community
"Now Let Us from the Table Rise" by Fred Kaan
"Be Not Afraid" by Robert J. Dufford
"The Battle Belongs to the Lord" by Jamie Owens-Collins
"Awesome God" by Rich Mullins

N. The Closing Communion Doxology

The concluding prayer of the Eucharist is a laudatory statement of praise. Following the primitive model of the

Jewish meal prayer, the prayer gives glory to God for God's provision; the people respond with the Amen. This concludes the worship at the Table with a strong note of praise. Here are several examples.

Traditional

> Through him, glory to thee, and honor, to the Father and to the Son, with the Holy Spirit, in the holy church, now and forever, Amen. (Hippolytus, *The Apostolic Tradition*)

Contemporary

> Eternal God, heavenly Father, you have graciously accepted us as living members of your Son our Savior Jesus Christ, and you have fed us with spiritual food in the Sacrament of his Body and Blood.
> Send us now into the world in peace, and grant us strength and courage to love and serve you with gladness and singleness of heart; through Christ our Lord. Amen. *(The Book of Common Prayer)*

INSTRUCTIONS FOR PREPARING THE CLOSING DOXOLOGY

DIRECTION	EXAMPLE
Begin with an ascription of praise.	Eternal God, heavenly Father,
Continue with a proclamation of what God has done for the congregation in the commu-nion.	You have graciously accepted us as living members of your Son, our Savior Jesus Christ, and you have fed us with spiritual food in the sacrament of his Body and Blood.
Continue with a request for	Send us now into the world in

God's continued presence in life and work.

peace, and grant us strength and courage to love and serve you with gladness and single-ness of heart;

End with an appropriate ascription.

Through Christ our Lord.

Guidelines for Planning Table Worship

1. Evaluate the content of your present Table Worship. Which of the New Testament terms below define your emphasis?

   - The Lord's Supper
   - Communion
   - Breaking of Bread
   - Eucharist

2. Does your Table worship express New Testament fullness, or is it lacking in one or more of the meanings of Communion? Mark below:

Emphasis on the Crucifixion   Yes ☐   No ☐
Emphasis on the Resurrection   Yes ☐   No ☐
Emphasis on Intimate Relationship Yes ☐   No ☐
Emphasis on Thanksgiving   Yes ☐   No ☐

3. Is the style of your worship traditional, contemporary, or blended?

4. Study Table H on page 146. Working with the space below, compare your worship with the normative pattern that is closest to your style. In the left column, write down the normative pattern. In the middle column write down your present order of Table worship.

In the column on the right make notes and comments on your proposed Table worship.

Normal pattern	Present order	Proposed order

5. Comment on the specific acts of worship in the proposed order above. Below is a list of all the elements of Table Worship. Check those that will be used and make notes that will help you think more clearly about the revised plan of Table Worship.

☐ Ascription of Praise _____

☐ Offertory Hymn _____

☐ Preparation of the Table _____

☐ The Exhortation and Examination of Conscience
_____
_____

☐ *Sursum Corda* _____

☐ *Sanctus* (Holy, Holy, Holy) _____

☐ The Prayer of Thanksgiving _____

☐ Prayer of Praise to the Father _____

☐ Song of Praise to the Father _____

☐ Thankfulness to the Son _____

☐ Invocation of the Holy Spirit _____

☐ Song to the Holy Spirit _____

☐ An Acclamation Song _____

☐ Breaking of the Bread _____

☐ Remembrance _____

☐ The Lamb of God Song _____

☐ Invitation to Receive _____

☐ Communion Songs _____

☐ Anointing of Oil _____

☐ Post-communion Song _____

☐ Doxology Prayer _____

6. Now that you have determined a possible content, structure, and style for your Table worship, think through the expected experience of the worshiper. In the column on the left, place your proposed order

of service. In the column on the right, comment on the experience of worship formed by the content, structure, and style of your design.

Proposed Order   Expected Experience

The Nature of the Alternative Time of Thanksgiving

Because not all churches celebrate the Eucharist weekly, an alternative act to communion emerged in many churches. It is generally agreed that the Service of the Word should always be followed by a response of some sort, and many churches are now experimenting with various responses that specifically give thanks to God for the work of Christ accomplished by the Crucifixion and the Resurrection.

There are, of course, many ways to respond to God, but specifically concerning the alternative time of thanksgiving, there are five kinds of response in addition to the Eucharist that many churches now practice.

First, there is the **sacred response.** With this, worship focuses on an invitation to receive Christ or a sacramental act, such as baptism; the commissioning of ministries within the Church; or for services of healing.

Second is the **sung response.** Some renewal worship communities sing for ten to twenty minutes in response to the Service of the Word. Here a congregation may weave together hymns and choruses that follow the pattern of the Eucharist prayer: songs in praise of the Father, songs remembering the work of the Son, and songs that invoke the presence of the

Holy Spirit. During these songs the ministry of anointing with oil and a prayer for healing may also be implemented.

Third is the **prayer response**. The prayer response focuses on prayers of intercession and thanksgiving. It may begin with a general prayer of thanksgiving that shifts the congregation from the Service of the Word to a time of prayer. Here a variety of forms of prayer may be used by the congregation.

A fourth kind of alternative response is the **interactive response**. This may include a response to the sermon in the form of a talk-back sermon. There is precedent to interactive sermons in the early Church and in the seventeenth and eighteenth centuries. Puritan worship contained a time of "witnessing" which engaged the community in the application of the Sunday sermon. The resurgence of the talk-back sermon can be a wonderful substitution to the monologue nature of many contemporary sermons.

Finally, churches are also engaging in an **action response**. An action response is directed primarily toward the work that the church does in the world. It may focus on the missionaries that are sponsored by the church or on the ministry of the church in the local neighborhoods (through soup kitchens, clothing drives, or other forms of service). Worship is not only what we do within the church; it is also our outreach, and thus brings outreach into the local church as a witness to the Word.

Suggested Structures for the Alternative Time of Thanksgiving

The alternative time of thanksgiving maintains the historical structure of Word followed by a response to the Word. However, when the alternative time of thanksgiving follows the Service of the Word, some adjustments may need to be made to maintain an appropriate flow of worship. (See Table I.)

TABLE I: THE FOURFOLD PATTERN WITH THE ALTERNATIVE RESPONSE

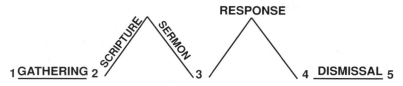

In order to maintain the flow of worship, use the transition times for transitional acts such as the passing of the peace, announcements, and offering:

1. Announcements may be given before the service.
2. The Passing of the Peace may occur at the end of the gathering.
3. A transitional song or prayer may move the congregation into the time of thanksgiving.
4. At the end of the service of thanksgiving one or more of the following acts may occur:
     * the passing of the peace.
     * the offering
     * the announcements
5. Conclude with the dismissal.

For example, some congregations desire to move into the main thanksgiving immediately following the sermon, placing parts such as the creed, the prayers, or the passing of the peace at different places in the order of worship. In this ordering of worship, it is important to maintain the flow of worship as well as its content. For this reason planners may want to move the congregation into the alternative time of thanksgiving with a transitional act of worship.

THE SACRED RESPONSE

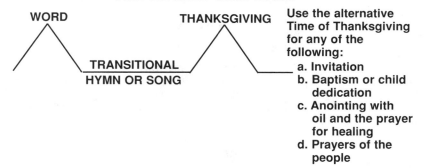

THE SUNG RESPONSE

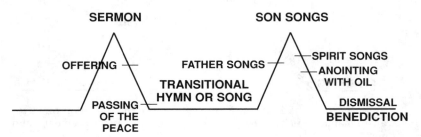

THE PRAYER RESPONSE

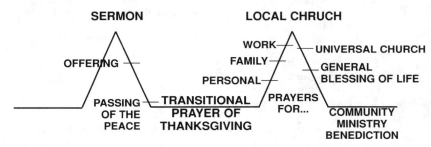

AN INTERACTIVE RESPONSE

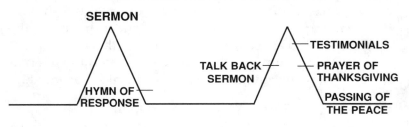

THE ACTION RESPONSE

The internal structure of each act of response is always determined by the content of the response; for example, a sung response will be structurally different from an action response. Be sensitive to flow and movement. Always ask, What kind of spiritual experience does this act order in the heart of the worshiper?

For planning the time of response, I have listed below the five suggested responses and have included some preliminary comments about the structure of each.

Music During the Alternative Time of Thanksgiving

The use of music in the alternative time of thanksgiving will be determined by the content of the specific response. Worship planners need to be sensitive, first of all, to the transition that moves the worship from the Service of the Word to the alternative response. Second, planners need to think through the flow of the alternative time of thanksgiving, so that it is not disrupted by a series of unconnected acts of worship. The alternative time of thanksgiving is not a program. It needs to be designed in such a way that a natural flow is established from beginning to end. (For example, do not make any announcements during this time.) Since the alternative service of thanksgiving can be conducted with an exciting amount of variety, it is not possible to be specific about the music. Follow the guidelines stated above and experiment with the use of music, remembering that music assists and serves the specific experience of the worshiper.

Resources for the Alternative Time of Thanksgiving

A. Prayers of Thanksgiving

One or more of the following prayers may be used, or the minister may pray an extemporaneous prayer following the pattern of one or more of the prayers below:

Almighty God, Father of all mercies, we your unworthy servants do give you most humble and hearty thanks for all your goodness and loving-kindness to us and to all people. We bless you for our creation, preservation, and all the blessings of this life; but above all, for your overflowing love in the redemption of the world by Jesus Christ; for the means of grace, and for the hope of glory. And we pray to you, give us a deep experience of all your mercies so that our hearts will be filled with thankfulness and that we may show forth your praise, not only with our lips, but also in our lives; by giving up ourselves to your service, and by walking before you in holiness and righteousness all our days; Through Jesus Christ our Lord, to whom, with you and the Holy Ghost, be all honor and glory, world without end. *Amen.*

B. A Litany of Thanksgiving

Prayers of thanksgiving may be spoken by the minister or worship leader, followed by a response from the people. The following litany prayer example structures a prayer, a response by the people, and a suggested concluding song:

Almighty God, you who are unchanging in your purpose of continuously blessing us; we acknowledge your many gifts, which you shower upon us from generation to generation. We give you thanks for the faith you have given us and for empowering us to share this faith with other peoples;

Response:
We give you thanks, O Lord.

or

I bid you to offer your prayers of thanks.

The people pray.

or

Sing "Give Thanks with a Grateful Heart"

Above all, we give thanks for the great salvation you have

made free to us in your blessed Son, our Savior; and for all the gifts of your grace bestowed and promised in him;

Response:
We give you thanks, O Lord.

or

I bid you to offer your prayer of thanks.

The people pray.

or

Great is thy faithfulness.

or

Grant that we may show forth our gratitude not only with our lips, but in our lives; by giving up ourselves to your service and by walking before you in holiness and righteousness all our days, through Jesus Christ our Lord, to whom be glory, world without end. Amen.

Response:
Sing "Alleluia, Alleluia," "Give Thanks," or "Wait for the Lord"

C. Songs for the Alternative Time of Thanksgiving

TRINITARIAN SONGS OF PRAISE

Hymns
"Glory to God, Glory in the Highest" Traditional *"Gloria in Excelsis"*
"I Bind unto Myself Today" by Saint Patrick, paraphrased by Cecil Alexander
"Praise the Lord! O Heavens, Adore Him" from The Foundling Hospital Collection
"Praise God from Whom" by Thomas Ken
"Sing to the Lord a New Song" by Hal Hopson
"Be Thou My Vision" traditional Irish hymn
"We Believe (in God the Father)" by Graham Kendrick

177

Choruses

"Magnify the Lord" by Bert Polman
"You Are My Hiding Place" by Michael Ledner
"The Lord Is My Light" the Taizé Community
"Glorify Your Name" by Donna Adkins
"I Love You Lord" by Laurie Klein
"We Bow Down" by Twila Paris
"Lord God, Almighty" by Coni Huisman
"I Exalt Thee" by Pete Sanchez Jr.

SONGS IN PRAISE OF THE FATHER

Hymns

"Great Is Thy Faithfulness" by Thomas O. Chisholm
"How Great Thou Art" by Stuart K. Hine
"Sing Praise to the Father" by Margaret Clarkson
"Of the Father's Love Begotten" by Marcus Aurelius C.
   Prudentius (fourth century)
"Praise the Lord Who Reigns Above" by Charles
   Wesley
"Give to Our God Immortal Praise" by Isaac Watts
"Sing of the Lord's Goodness" by Ernest Sands
"To God Be the Glory" by Fanny Crosby

Choruses

"Worthy, You Are Worthy" by Don Moen
"When I Look into Your Holiness" by Wayne and
   Cathy Perrin
"Awesome God" by Rich Mullins
"How Majestic Is Your Name" by Michael W. Smith
"Ah, Lord God" by Kay Chance
"Praise to You, O God of Mercy" by Marty Haugen
"Blessed Be the Name of the Lord" by Don Moen
"There's No God as Great" traditional Spanish song

SONGS TO REMEMBER THE WORK OF THE SON

Hymns

"Join All the Glorious Names" by Isaac Watts
"Amazing Grace" by John Henry Newton

178

"My Jesus, I Love Thee" by William R. Featherstone
"At the Name of Jesus" by Caroline M. Noel
"Ah, Holy Jesus" by Johann Heermann
"Alleluia, Sing to Jesus" by William C. Dix
"Crown Him with Many Crowns" by Matthew Bridges

Choruses
"Give Thanks with a Grateful Heart" by Henry Smith
"The King of Glory" by W. F. Jabusch
"King of Kings" by Naomi-Batya and Sophie Conty
"Alleluia, Alleluia! Give Thanks" by Donald Fishel
"Jesus Is Our King" by Sherrell Prebble and Howard Clark
"We See the Lord" anonymous
"Soon and Very Soon" by Andraé Crouch
"Wait for the Lord" the Taizé Community

SONGS INVOKING THE HOLY SPIRIT

Hymns
"Like the Murmur of the Dove's Song" by Carl P. Daw Jr.
"There's a Spirit in the Air" by Brian Wren
"Creating Spirit, Holy Lord" translated by Ralph Wright
"Be Still, for the Spirit of the Lord" by Dave Evans
"Holy Spirit, Mighty God" by Calvin Seerveld
"Speak, Lord, in the Stillness" by E. May Grimes
"Spirit of the Living God" by Daniel Iverson

Choruses
"Come, Holy Spirit" by Mark Foreman
"Now Holy Spirit, Ever One" by Ambrose of Milan
"Spirit Song" by John Wimber
"Surely the Presence of the Lord" by Lanny Wolfe
"Come into His Presence" anonymous
"Create in Me a Clean Heart, O God" anonymous

Guidelines for Planning the Alternative Time of Thanksgiving

1. Briefly describe the general nature of the alternative time of thanksgiving.

_____

_____

_____

_____

2. Which of the following alternative thanks would you like to incorporate into the worship of your church?

- sacred response

- sung response

- prayer response

- interactive response

- action response

3. In the space below, plan an alternative time of thanksgiving. Indicate the proposed order in the left column and your expected experience of the worshiper in the right column.

PROPOSED ORDER   EXPECTED EXPERIENCE

4. Examine your proposed order and answer the following:

Have you suggested an appropriate way to transition from the Word to the alternative time of thanksgiving?

Yes ☐   No ☐

Is there an internal flow to the acts of worship you have planned in the body of the alternative time of thanksgiving?

Yes ☐   No ☐

Have the announcements been placed in an open space of worship so that they do not interrupt the flow?

Yes ☐   No ☐

Is the passing of the peace in an open space of worship that will not disrupt the flow?

Yes ☐   No ☐

Is the offering in a place of response and integrated into worship as part of the flow?

Yes ☐   No ☐

5. Experiment. Because the alternative time of thanksgiving is a new development in worship, and because there are a variety of practices, you will need to experiment with the various forms of alternative thanksgiving until you have found the content, structure, and style most appropriate within your church community.

Chapter 5

The Service of the Dismissal: Going Forth to Love and Serve the Lord

The Lord bless us and keep us,
the Lord make his face to shine upon us,
and be gracious unto us, the Lord lift up the light of his
countenance upon us and give us peace.

TRADITIONAL BLESSING BASED ON PSALM 67 (SEVENTH CENTURY)

The Nature of the Dismissal

Paul captured the essence of being commissioned from worship when he wrote to the Roman Christians: "Therefore, I urge you, brothers, in view of God's mercy, to offer your bodies as living sacrifices, holy and pleasing to God—this is your spiritual act of worship" (Romans 12:1). Paul espoused the idea that worship is a way of life. Rather than ending at the door of the church, worship continues into every aspect of our lives—into our home, our work, and even our leisure.

This thought is captured in *The Book of Common Prayer.* The service ends with the minister saying, "Let us go forth into the world rejoicing in the power of the Spirit." The people enthusiastically respond, "Thanks be to God." Again, in the Catholic *Constitution on the Sacred Liturgy:* "The Liturgy is the summit toward which the activity of the church is directed; at the same time, it is the fount from which all the church's power flows" (I.10). These two documents echo the Pauline concept that worship extends to all of life and to all that we do. For this reason, we need to think clearly about what we do when we send forth the congregation.

If we want the Dismissal to mean more to the worshiper, we need to begin by asking the simple question, What should the Dismissal do? Primarily, the Dismissal is a blessing. In worship, we actually bless God when we offer praise and worship. To bless God means that we pronounce or confer upon God the wonder and might of God's own name. When we bless God through our praise and worship, however, we do not confer anything on God. Rather, we bless God by doing what is pleasing to God—acknowledging and serving God.

In contrast, when God blesses us, God confers on us a power to fulfill our calling in righteousness and holiness in Jesus Christ. God's blessing on us is a gift—an actual pouring out on us of the Holy Spirit. This notion of God pouring out a blessing on us is found in the Old Testament Aaronic blessing:

> The LORD bless you and keep you; the LORD make his face shine upon you and be gracious to you; the LORD turn his face toward you and give you peace. (Numbers 6:24-26)

The key to this and all other biblical blessings is found in verse 27: *"So they will put my name on the Israelites"* [italics mine]. In a blessing, God confers the divine name on us, and that is how we are to live our lives. I wonder how our lives would change if in every detail of our daily life we consciously recognized, "I have the name of God upon me!"

The Structure of the Dismissal

The structure of the Dismissal is shaped by its contents. It simply brings closure to public worship and sends the people forth to continue worship in their lives. Three actions accomplish this content, actions that are common to traditional, contemporary, or blended communities:

- The Benediction (God's blessing)
- A Dismissal hymn (a hymn or gospel song that sends the people forth with a mission)
- Words of Dismissal

Although announcements may be a part of the Dismissal, the first liturgical act of the Dismissal is the blessing, or Benediction. In the liturgical tradition, the pastor stretches forth his or her right hand and, forming a gesture symbolizing the cross, speaks the words of Dismissal. The people repeat the sign of the cross and respond with the *Amen*. In contemporary worship, the minister will raise his or her hands above the head, a gesture that symbolizes the laying on of hands, and say the Benediction to the people as they stand. They respond *Amen*.

In worship renewal today a significant emphasis is placed on the importance of recapturing the true meaning of the Benediction. When the blessing is pronounced, the people are asked to stand to receive the blessing as a conscious, personal declaration from God. Some pastors are weaving brief references to specific aspects of life (work, leisure, and so forth) into the blessing so that the worshiper may be reminded that God is present in every aspect of daily life. The blessing is then followed by a hymn or song of being sent forth into the world. It is most appropriate to sing a hymn of commissioning that touches on service, mission, or the Christian life. Gospel songs fit well as recessional hymns.

During the hymn, leaders of worship recess to the back of the sanctuary. In the liturgical tradition, the order of recessing is the same as the order of the procession:

- the cross bearer (if a cross is used)
- banner carriers (if banners are used)
- Scripture readers
- choir
- ministers

The ministers, during the Dismissal, gather at the back of the sanctuary, where they lead the singing of the final hymn and then conclude with the words of Dismissal. These words bring closure to the worship experience and connect worship with the worshiper's life in the world. A common form of closure is as follows: the final hymn has been sung; the minister, worship leaders, and choir are at the back of the church; the minister or a layperson lifts hands and cries, "Go forth into the world to love and serve the Lord." The people then respond with an enthusiastic, "Thanks be to God! Alleluia!"

The Experience of the Worshiper in the Dismissal

Although the Dismissal is the shortest act of worship, we should not assume that it makes little impact on the worshiper. In fact, if the preceding parts of worship accomplish what they are intended to do, the closing acts of worship should be characterized by an experience of resolve. When the blessing is pronounced, the worshiper ought to experience the empowering presence of God and may resolve to continue to live life in this presence. The same may be said for the Dismissal hymn and the closing words. They reiterate the notion that we have been sent forth by God, who remains with us.

Resources for the Dismissal

A. Examples of the Benediction

May the grace of the Lord Jesus Christ, and the love of God, and the fellowship of the Holy Spirit be with you all. Amen. (2 Corinthians 13:14) or

The peace of God, which passes all understanding, keep you hearts and minds in the knowledge and love of God, and of God's Son Jesus Christ our Lord; and the blessing of God almighty, the Father, the Son, and the Holy Spirit, remain with you always. Amen.

B. Examples of Dismissal Hymns and Songs

Hymns
"Jesus Shall Reign" by Isaac Watts
"Lift High the Cross" by George W. Kitchin
"Lead On, O King Eternal" by Ernest W. Shurtleff
"Christ for the World We Sing" by Samuel Wolcott
"Christ Is Alive" by Brian Wren
"God of Grace and God of Glory" by Harry E. Fosdick
"Lord, You Give the Great Commission" by Jeffery
    Rowthorn
"Sent Forth by God's Blessing" by Omer Westendorf

Choruses
"The Trees of the Field" by Steffi Geiser Rubin
"Song for the Nations" by Chris Christensen
"Send Us Out" by John Michael Talbot
"We Are Marching in the Light of the Lord" traditional
    Zulu song
"Send Me Jesus (*Thuma mina*)" a South African song

C. The Words of Dismissal

The words of Dismissal are words of closure and commissioning. From the back of the congregation the minister ends public worship with a proclamation that begins the Christian service in the world for the following week. An example may be: "Go in peace to love and serve the Lord," to which the people respond, "Thanks be to God."

Examples of the Words of Dismissal

Go out into the world in peace;
have courage;

187

hold on to what is good;
return no one evil for evil;
strengthen the faint-hearted;
support the weak, and help the suffering;
honor everyone;
love and serve the Lord,
rejoicing in the power of the Holy Spirit.
(1 Corinthians 16:13; 2 Timothy 2:1; Ephesians 6:10;
1 Thessalonians 5:13-22; 1 Peter 2:17)

or

Be watchful,
stand firm in your faith,
be courageous, be strong.
Let all that you do be done in love.
(1 Corinthians 16:13-14 RSV)

or

Whatever you do, in word or deed, do everything in the name of the Lord Jesus, giving thanks to God the Father through him. (Colossians 3:17 NRSV)

or

Go in peace to serve the Lord, in the name of Christ.
Thanks be to God. [Alleluia, Alleluia.]

D. Variation in the Dismissal

There is very little variety that can or should be done in the Dismissal. The Dismissal is best kept succinct and brief, serving the function of sending the people forth. Nevertheless, here are several suggestions that can enhance the Dismissal:

DANCE

Use a dance during the Dismissal hymn. During the recessional God transcends the congregation and is experienced as the One who goes before the church, leading people into the world to serve the gospel. When the Dismissal hymn is choreographed for dance and led by a dancer, the movement itself can be a powerful spiritual experience of going into the world with the God who goes before us.

SPECIAL MUSIC

Have the choir sing a special selection from the back of the church. This approach is very effective during festive seasons. For example, the Dismissal on the last Sunday after Epiphany may be characterized by a "Farewell to the Alleluias," since the Alleluias will not be sung again until Easter. This "Farewell to the Alleluias" serves the Paschal Event in an eschatological way, creating a memory during Lent that creates a longing for the Resurrection (symbolized by the eventual return of the Alleluia).

CLAPPING

In contemporary churches the congregation may end worship with several celebration choruses followed by clapping. The clap is for God and expresses the joy of having been in the presence of God.

Guidelines for Planning the Dismissal

1. Summarize the purpose of the Dismissal.

2. How does your present worship accomplish (or not accomplish) the purpose of the Dismissal?

3. In the space below, compare the content of your Dismissal with the universal pattern; then, in the column on the right, jot down the changes you intend to make in the Dismissal.

Universal Pattern   Current Dismissal   Proposed Changes

Benediction

Song of
    Dismissal

Closing
    Words

189

Appendixes

Appendix I

Planning Blended Worship only contains enough prayers and songs to give you both a taste of traditional and adequate instructions for writing contemporary material. I strongly suggest this book be supplemented by two additional resources: a prayer book and a book of hymns and songs. I recommend *The Book of Common Prayer* (Episcopal), *The Book of Common Worship* (Presbyterian), and *The United Methodist Book of Worship*. Any of these prayer books will provide you with numerous additional resources. I also suggest you purchase a blended song book containing both old and new traditions. Four such publications are *Renew! Songs and Hymns for Blended Worship* (Hope); *Gather, Comprehensive Edition* (GIA); *Glory and Praise*, second edition (Oregon Catholic Press); and *Celebration Hymnal* (Integrity/Hosanna/Word). (As a helpful reference, most songs referred to in *Planning Blended Worship* are found in *Renew! Songs and Hymns for Blended Worship*.)

Announcements

The question most frequently asked in my workshops is, Where do you place the announcements? The most important principle to keep in mind regarding the announcements is that they need to be presented at a time when they will not disrupt the flow of worship. They need to be placed where there is a natural transition from one set of worship acts to another. There are three such spaces in the fourfold pattern, as indicated in the following graph:

190

THE ALTERNATIVE RESPONSE

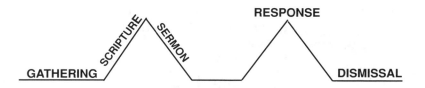

1. Announcements may be given before worship begins.

2. Announcements may be given after the Service of the Word, following the Passing of the Peace. At this point there is a normal break in the flow before the beginning of the Eucharist. However, announcements should not be presented at this time if you are using the Alternative Time of Thanksgiving since this time usually flows straight out of the sermon without a stop in the flow of worship.

3. Announcements may be given during the Dismissal, just prior to the Benediction. If you have just celebrated the Eucharist, a space of silence should probably precede the announcements.

The Offering

Since the very beginning of Christian worship, the offering has been considered a response to the Service of the Word. It is not merely putting money into a plate; it is a genuine act of worship. In the early Church an offering of food was made between the end of the Service of the Word and the beginning of the Eucharist. As the bread and wine were brought to the Table, foodstuffs were also brought, later to be given to the poor. The food offering slowly disappeared with the introduction of a primarily money-based economy, and eventually an offering plate was introduced.

African American worship offers an interesting and challenging approach to the offering. The giving of tithes and offerings is a high point during worship. In many churches the offering plate is placed on a table in the front, and the entire congregation processes to the front to present their gifts. This approach makes the offering more participatory and provides a time for the experience of joy in giving. The offering may also be conducted during the Alternative Time of Thanksgiving.

Appendix II:
Practical Tools for Planners

The Stages of Worship Renewal

In the past several decades, the research of educational specialists has made it increasingly clear that progress, development, and change occur in stages. The work of Piaget and Kohlberg in moral development, as well as that of James Fowler in religious development, has been helpful in understanding the sequence of change. What is true in the field of moral and spiritual development appears to be true in the area of worship renewal: growth happens in stages. Evidence for these stages arises out of the work of pastors and church leaders who have committed themselves to a worship renewal based on biblical and historical precedent. These studies suggest seven stages of development, which a local church passes through in its pursuit of growth in worship:

1. Awareness Stage
2. Analysis Stage
3. Knowledge Stage
4. Resourcing Stage
5. Experimental Stage
6. Renewal Stage
7. *Semper reformada*

The steps toward worship renewal are critical stages that must unfold in sequence. Obviously there is no set time frame for concluding one stage and entering another. Instead, the stages of development merge into one another, interconnecting and supporting one another. Furthermore, in any given community at any given time, people will be at different stages of development. Once a sizable portion of the congregation has passed through these phases, leaders need to be sensitive to those who are at other stages of development in their spiritual journeys.

The process of growth takes time, whether it be the growth of a tree, a child, or a church. The process requires patience. Each stage may be enjoyed for what it offers. It is cause for celebration when renewal efforts in worship bear fruit in which meaning and joy are tied to a reenactment of God's saving acts and in which God's people are touched with transforming power.

The Awareness Stage. The initial step toward worship renewal begins when part, or all, of a congregation senses there is more to worship than their present experience. This is the work of the Holy Spirit. Such awareness is often prompted by a visit to another church where worship is experienced in a deeper dimension or through contact with a person, an article, or a book that challenges one's experience and concept of worship. This exposure usually results in a more intense interest in worship, demonstrated through noncritical questioning and a subsequent longing for a more fulfilled worship.

The Analysis Stage. The second stage of development grows out of the unfulfilled longing for the more satisfying worship that was experienced or encountered in the first stage. Initially, a person or community begins to ache for a true experience of worship. There is an unquenchable need for something more. Because a person does not know what that "something more" is, and because the church is not moving beyond a worship now regarded by some as dead, the inner-self becomes frustrated and upset. Attendance at worship often becomes counterproductive. At this point, when the worshiper begins to reject the worship in his or her church, several things may happen: the person may reject the style of worship but remain in silent protest, or he or she may openly criticize what is experienced as shallow and irrelevant worship. Finally, the person may explode in unresolved anger and leave the church, looking for another community where the longing for a deeper experience of worship may be fulfilled.

For this reason, it is important for a local church to implement a critical evaluation and feedback survey, which examines every aspect of worship and allows for honest input from every member: (1) The worshiper, feeling involved in the future direction of worship, will be less likely to leave the church in search of another worshiping community. (2) A diagnostic tool will bring to the surface hidden talents among worshipers which may be put to work. (3) A diagnostic survey will provide the church staff with a sense of the congregation's disposition toward worship renewal. It may give the leadership permission to move more quickly toward worship renewal or caution them to adopt a slower, more deliberate pace. (4) A diagnostic should pique the interest of both the leadership and the congregation toward the next stage of development.

The Knowledge Stage. The first two stages are subjective phases of development that occur in varying degrees among churches. The knowledge stage is an objective period of development. The field of knowledge that touches upon worship is vast and includes knowledge of the biblical, historical, and theological sources of worship; learning in the arts; some understanding of communication theory; and sensitivity to ways to introduce change. Furthermore, all of this knowledge has to be distilled and adapted to the particularities of a specific denomination or tradition. Renewed worship needs to express what is common to the Church universal, but in a style also acceptable to the local church. And finally, this is all made more complex by the fact that knowledge alone is not adequate. Each church must rely on the Holy Spirit to give life to this learning.

During this stage a congregation may be most tempted to give up on the seven-step process and opt for the quick fix. If worship renewal is seen merely as learning a few new songs or introducing more of the arts, then a minimum amount of knowledge is needed. The principle and practices of worship that arise out of the gospel and the biblical-historical practice of the Church represents a serious discipline of study every bit as demanding as biblical studies or theology.

A congregation deeply desiring renewal of worship with staying power cannot afford to bypass the stages of learning. Because there is such a voluminous amount of data available, it is best for a church to have both an introductory course on worship and an ongoing study that continues to explore various facets of corporate celebration.

The Resourcing Stage. The period of gathering material for worship renewal begins after a certain amount of knowledge has been acquired. Like the gathering of information, this resourcing will continue as the church grows gradually. As a congregation becomes more knowledgeable about worship, the how-to question will naturally arise, creating the demand for a variety of resources to assist a congregation in its worship growth.

In the past decade, a virtual torrent of materials, prayers, confessions, Eucharist liturgies, sacramental actions, music, art, and dance has appeared. In addition, an equally impressive number of studies and resources has been published dealing with the church year and the relation of worship to evangelism, education, and spirituality. A church may want to acquire *The Complete Library of Christian Worship* (Hendrickson) as a helpful beginning reference guide.

The Experimentation Stage. Experimentation with new forms of worship can be introduced slowly in connection with the two previous stages. Unfortunately, some churches leap to this stage with inadequate knowledge and resourcing. When this happens, a congregation may quickly revert to the style of worship they were using before. They failed to construct an adequate foundation for making permanent change.

The Renewal Stage. The most important hour of the week for a congregation is the hour it gathers for worship. When the people are no longer passive spectators but active worshipers, statement like "I love to worship" and "This worship strengthens me" will be heard time and time again.

Genuine renewed worship occurs when God's event of salvation in Jesus Christ is genuinely celebrated and is truly experienced as a healing event by all who gather. People go home from worship not frustrated or angry, but at peace. They will know that God is there for them, that Jesus Christ is actually present in worship to touch them, to heal them, and to make them whole.

Semper Reformada. Keeping renewal alive requires the continuing engagement of the congregation in the process that has been described. Once a congregation has passed through these various stages and entered a state of worship renewal, it is of utmost importance that the congregation remain diligent and watchful in its practice of worship. The Protestant reformers had a phrase for this activity: *semper reformada* ("always reforming").

How to Set Up a Planning Ministry

A worship ministry is a group, arranged from the church staff and congregation, that encourages the continual improvement of worship through prayerful planning, thoughtful evaluation, and constant attention to the process whereby a worshiping community is formed. Follow the steps below to establish a planning ministry in the local church.

STEP ONE: ESTABLISH A CORE GROUP OF PEOPLE COMMITTED TO WORSHIP RENEWAL.

A church that is seeking renewal needs a core of godly people deeply committed to seeing worship come alive. The kind of worship we want in our church grows out of the spiritual life of the congregation and feeds back into that life. If many of the people in the church are spiritually dead, unconverted, or indifferent to the gospel, the task of worship renewal will be more difficult. Nevertheless, a small core of committed people who begin to pray for worship renewal and begin taking measures toward it can have a significant effect on an entire congregation. This group should meet on a regular basis, weekly if possible, and certainly not less than once a month.

STEP TWO: IDENTIFY ONE PERSON WHO HAS THE CALLING FOR WORSHIP RENEWAL.

There needs to be one person in a leadership position who is committed to bringing the renewal of worship. Worship renewal is not finding a few new gimmicks that will give people a religious high. Rather, worship renewal is a matter that requires considerable understanding and sensitive, wise leadership. No one person can know everything about all of the subjects of worship renewal, yet to make worship renewal a reality, there has to be one person who has some sensitivity to all the fields of study from which worship draws. This person may be the pastor, the music director, or a layperson. Whoever emerges as this leader must have a sense of calling to this ministry and the respect and cooperation of those who work with him or her.

STEP THREE: ESTABLISH A TEAM OF WORSHIP MINISTERS.

A team of worship ministers has two basic responsibilities. The first is to plan everything related to worship—and the planning of worship is not limited to the *order* of worship itself.

197

Although that is certainly a central task of the worship ministers, other responsibilities include such matters as the worship environment, hospitality, music, drama, and technical concerns.

The second responsibility of the worship ministers is weekly evaluation. Each service must be evaluated, preferably within twenty-four hours of the service. Planning worship is only half of the cycle. If worship is not evaluated on a regular basis, it will soon fall back into the old pattern, or else the new pattern will become established and lose its vitality. The committee must pay constant attention to worship through regular critical evaluation of all its parts.

Planning team size. The size of the worship ministry team will differ depending on the size and preferences of the congregation. Generally, in a smaller but growing church, a three-person ministry team is sufficient. In larger churches, the worship ministry team may consist of four persons who administer four groups of people related to the ministry of worship. The two configurations below are not set in stone. A congregation should feel free to experiment with the development of a team of worship ministers to find a configuration that works for it.

The team of worship ministers in the growing church. In a smaller but growing church, the makeup of the team of worship ministers is generally no more than three persons: the minister of oversight, the minister of music and the arts, and the minister of housekeeping:

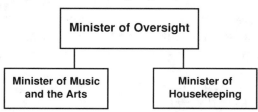

Minister of Oversight. Responsibilities include teaching worship, planning worship (with the other two ministers), and leading worship (or designating leadership).

Minister of Music and the Arts. Responsibilities include oversight of all choirs and musical groups, the lay reader's group (scripture readers, dramatists, dancers), and environmental art (seating, banners, flowers, and so on).

Minister of Housekeeping. Responsibilities include supervision of the church bulletin, hospitality, preparation for the Communion, and technical matters.

The team of worship ministers in the larger church. In a larger church, the team of worship ministers is an expanded version of the same ministry in the smaller church. It includes a minister of oversight, a minister of leadership, a minister of music and the arts, and a minister of housekeeping who acts in a capacity of leadership over the various ministries involved in worship.

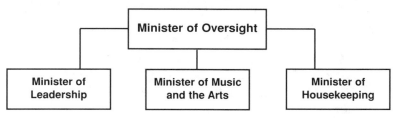

Minister of Oversight. This person coordinates the work of all the ministers of worship.

Minister of Leadership. This person coordinates all the work of the ministers of leadership. The minister of leadership may also fulfill the work of one or more of the following three ministries:

Teacher of Worship. Assumes responsibility to study worship, to teach a worship class, and provide educational input and resources for the other ministries listed below.

Planner of Worship. Actually plans the worship service, drawing on the input, expertise and talent of the other ministries listed below.

Leader of Worship. Actually leads the congregation in worship.

Minister of Music and the Arts. This person coordinates music, drama, dance and environmental art.

The Music Minister. Oversees all the musical groups in the church, such as choirs, soloists, cantors and instrumental groups, and integrates their contributions to worship with the other ministries.

The Drama Minister. Oversees all groups related to communication, such as the scripture readers' group and drama group, and integrates their ministry into worship.

The Environment Minister. Oversees the setting of worship, such as the seating arrangement; the use of flowers and plants; and especially the visual symbols used during the seasons of the church year: banners, cloths, and vestments. These matters are carefully related to the other ministries.

Minister of Housekeeping. Coordinates all the ministries that surround and support the ministry of worship.

Bulletin Minister. Collects all the materials necessary for the bulletin and coordinates the publication of the material.

Hospitality Minister. Provides directions for those who are called to create a hospitable environment for the worshiper through the work of greeting, ushering, coffee fellowship, and follow-up contacts.

Table Minister. Assumes responsibility for the demands related to the Table of the Lord, such as the communion ware, bread and wine, tablecloths, as well as preparation and cleanup duties.

Technical Minister. Oversees the purchase, care and use of microphones, recording equipment, and other technical matters related to worship.

STEP FOUR: EVALUATE WORSHIP WEEKLY.

The weekly evaluation of worship is indispensable to the process whereby a committee of worship ministers is able to bring about the renewal of worship. Each of the ministry areas may be evaluated by the entire committee of ministers at the beginning of each meeting. (See *The Complete Library of Christian Worship*, vol. 3, pp. 424-26.)

A Worship Planner

The following charts will be useful to worship committees for generating ideas for worship services, for planning services, and for evaluating services. In the spaces below, jot down all comments that are necessary for this service:

Date _____

Season of the year _____

Sunday _____

Sunday morning _____

Sunday evening _____

Midweek theme _____

Other _____

_____

Biblical texts _____

_____

_____

_____

Theme _____

_____

STEP 1: *BRAINSTORMING*

Take time to discuss the role of music, the arts, and housekeeping matters by using the following:

Music: Organ, piano, guitar, synthesizer, band, orchestra, hymns, choruses, psalms, anthems, solo, other.

The Arts: Scripture readers, drama group, dance, environmental art, seating, seasonal banners, cloths, vestments, visual symbols, other.

Housekeeping: Bulletin, greeters, ushers, coffee fellowship, follow-up, communion responsibilities, technical.

STEP 2: *FORMING THE SERVICE—PLANNING THE FOURFOLD PATTERN*

Select and order the material below in keeping with the style of worship desired.

Planning the Gathering

What acts will best bring the people into the presence of God? Informal singing, prelude, instrumental music, informal greetings, announcements, words of welcome, rehearsal of congregational music, entrance hymn, procession, greeting, invocations, acts of praise, confession and acts of pardon, opening prayer, the arts, the passing of the peace?

ORDER	COMMENTS
_____	_____
_____	_____
_____	_____
_____	_____
_____	_____
_____	_____
_____	_____

Planning the Service of the Word: How to Best Communicate God's Word

Scripture Readings: Old Testament, Epistle, Gospel.

Responses: psalms, choruses, canticles, hymns.

Responses to the Word: creed, hymn, talk-back sermon, invitation.

Prayer of the People, Passing of the Peace, Offering, Other.

ORDER   COMMENTS

_____   _____

_____   _____

_____   _____

_____   _____

_____   _____

Planning the Service of Thanksgiving: Ordering the Congregation's Response

Thanks with Table

Communion with lifting of hearts, preface prayer, *Sanctus*, prayer of thanksgiving, words of institution, words of remembrance, proclamation of the mystery of faith, prayer for the Holy Spirit, invitation to receive bread and wine, manner of reception (sit or go forward), communion song, anointing with oil, closing prayer.

ORDER   COMMENTS

_____   _____

_____   _____

_____   _____

_____   _____

_____   _____

Thanks without the Table

Sacred action, sung response, interactive response, action response.

ORDER	COMMENTS
_____	_____
_____	_____
_____	_____
_____	_____
_____	_____
_____	_____

Planning the Service of Dismissal: How to Send the People Forth into Mission

Announcements, Benediction, Dismissal hymn, words of Dismissal.

ORDER	COMMENTS
_____	_____
_____	_____
_____	_____
_____	_____
_____	_____
_____	_____

STEP 3: EVALUATING WORSHIP

Go over each part of the service, evaluating strengths, weaknesses, and ways to improve.

The Spatial and Environmental Setting

STRENGTHS   WEAKNESSES   NEED FOR
IMPROVEMENT

_____   _____   _____

_____   _____   _____

_____   _____   _____

_____   _____   _____

The Order and Flow of Worship

STRENGTHS   WEAKNESSES   NEED FOR
IMPROVEMENT

_____   _____   _____

_____   _____   _____

_____   _____   _____

_____   _____   _____

Music and the Arts: How well did they service the text of Worship?

STRENGTHS   WEAKNESSES   NEED FOR
IMPROVEMENT

_____   _____   _____

_____   _____   _____

_____   _____   _____

_____   _____   _____

(Adapted from *The Complete Library of Christian Worship*, vol. 3, pp. 426-28.)

Bibliography

Reference Works

Davies, J. G., ed. *The New Westminster Dictionary of Liturgy and Worship*. Philadelphia: Westminster, 1986.

Fink, Peter E., ed. *The New Dictionary of Sacramental Worship*. Collegeville, Minn.: Liturgical Press, 1990.

Lang, Jovian P. *Dictionary of the Liturgy*. New York: Catholic Book Publishing, 1989.

Thompson, Bard. *A Bibliography of Christian Worship*. The American Theological Library Association Monograph No. 25. Metuchen, N.J.: Scarecrow Press, 1989.

Webber, Robert, ed. *The Complete Library of Christian Worship*. 7 vols. Peabody, Mass.: Hendrickson, 1993.

White, James F. *Documents of Christian Worship*. Louisville: Westminster/John Knox Press, 1992.

Books for Personal and Group Study by Robert Webber

Learning to Worship with All Your Heart: A Study in the Biblical Foundations of Christian Worship. Peabody, Mass.: Hendrickson, 1996.

Rediscovering the Missing Jewel: A Study in Worship Through the Centuries. Peabody, Mass.: Hendrickson, 1997.

Renew Your Worship: A Study in Blending of Traditional and Contemporary Worship. Peabody, Mass.: Hendrickson, 1996.

Enter His Courts with Praise: A Study of the Role of Music and the Arts in Worship. Peabody, Mass.: Hendrickson, 1996.

Rediscovering the Christian Feasts: A Study in the Services of the Christian Year. Peabody, Mass.: Hendrickson, 1996.

Encountering the Healing Power of God: A Study in the Sacred Actions of Worship. Peabody, Mass.: Hendrickson, 1996.

Empowered by the Holy Spirit: A Study in the Ministries of Worship. Peabody, Mass.: Hendrickson, 1996.

Prayer Book Resources

Book of Worship: United Church of Christ. Cleveland: United Church of Christ, Office for Church Life and Leadership, 1986.

The Book of Common Worship. Louisville: Westminster/John Knox Press, 1993.

The Daily Prayer Book. New York: Hebrew Publishing, 1995.

The Sacramentary. New York: Catholic Book Publishing, 1985.

Service Book of the Holy Orthodox-Catholic Apostolic Church. Englewood, N.J.: Antiochean Orthodox Christian Archdiocese of North America, 1983.

The United Methodist Book of Worship. Nashville: The United Methodist Publishing House, 1992.

General Resources

Austin, Gerard, et al. *Eucharist: Toward the Third Millennium.* Chicago: Liturgy Training Press, 1997.

Dawn, Marva J. *Reaching Out Without Dumbing Down.* Grand Rapids, Mich.: Eerdmans, 1995.

Foley, Edward. *From Age to Age.* Chicago: Liturgy Training Press, 1992.

Leisch, Barry. *The New Worship.* Grand Rapids, Mich.: Baker, 1996.

Martin, Ralph. *Worship in the Early Church.* Rev. ed. Grand Rapids, Mich.: Eerdmans, 1975.

Old, Hughes. *Leading in Prayer: A Workbook for Worship.* Grand Rapids, Mich.: Eerdmans, 1995.

Peterson, David. *Engaging with God: A Biblical Theology of Worship.* Grand Rapids, Mich: Eerdmans, 1993.

Schmemann, Alexander. *The Eucharist: Sacrament of the Kingdom.* New York: St. Vladimir's Press, 1988.

Taft, Robert. *Beyond East and West: Problems in Liturgical Understanding.* Washington: Pastoral Press, 1984.

Webber, Robert. *Worship Old and New.* 2d ed. Grand Rapids, Mich.: Zondervan, 1994.

White, James. *Introduction to Christian Worship.* 2d ed. Nashville: Abingdon Press, 1990.

Music and the Arts

Music

Celebration Hymnal: Songs and Hymns of Worship. Mobile, Ala.: Integrity Hosanna/Word Publishing, 1997.

Gather: Comprehensive Edition. Chicago: GIA, 1994.

Glory and Praise. 2d ed. Portland, Ore.: Catholic Press, 1997.

Renew! Songs and Hymns for Blended Worship. Carol Stream, Ill.: Hope Publishing Company, 1995.

The New Metrical Psalter. New York: The Church Hymnal Corporation, 1988.

Arts

Driver, Tom F. *The Magic of Ritual.* 2d ed. San Francisco: HarperSF, 1992.

Hickman, Hoyt, et al. *Handbook of the Christian Year.* 2d ed. Nashville: Abingdon Press, 1992.

Litherland, Janet. *Getting Started in Drama Ministry.* Colorado Springs: Meriwether Publishing, 1987.

Mauch, Marchita. *Shaping a House for the Church.* Chicago: Liturgical Training Press, 1990.

McComiskey, Thomas Edward. *Reading Scriptures in Public: A Guide for Preachers and Lay Readers.* Grand Rapids, Mich.: Baker, 1991.

Rosser, Aelred R. *A Well-Trained Tongue.* Chicago: Liturgical Training Press, 1996.

Smith, Judy Gattis. *Drama Through the Church Year.* Colorado Springs: Meriwether Publishing, 1984.

Vosko, Richard. *Through the Eye of a Rose Window: A Perspective on the Environment for Worship.* San Jose, Calif.: Resource Publications, 1981.